Part of me grew envious of classmates with doting boyfriends.

I was happy my sisters shared the company of thoughtful black men, but seeing them together made me feel lonelier than ever. Would I ever be in the same position, or forever immersed in solitude? I had a hard enough time relating to other women. Talking to men was out of the question. Missing from my teenage years were the usual rites of passage—crushes on boys, holding hands at the movies or kissing at the school dance. I feared I would be a lonely old biddy for the rest of my life.

A Background Note about
Learning to Live:
A Black Woman's Journey Beyond Foster Care

More than half a million children in the United States are living in foster care. Most are eventually reunited with their families. But some, like Theresa Cameron, spend their lives being passed from one foster home to another. They grow up without ever having the comfort of a family's love, or even the security of knowing, in a very elementary way, who they are. Being deprived of such a basic sense of identity leaves deep and lasting scars—scars that people who have not experienced such loss can hardly imagine. Thanks to Theresa's expressive words, we have a record of one extraordinary woman's journey to confront her pain and heal her wounds.

THERESA CAMERON

Learning to Live:

A Black Woman's Journey Beyond Foster Care

TP THE TOWNSEND LIBRARY

LEARNING TO LIVE
A Black Woman's Journey
Beyond Foster Care

TP THE TOWNSEND LIBRARY

For more titles in the Townsend Library,
visit our website: **www.townsendpress.com**

All new material in this edition is
copyright © 2009 by Townsend Press.
Printed in the United States of America

0 9 8 7 6 5 4 3 2 1

Illustrations copyright © 2009 by Hal Taylor

Townsend Press, Inc.
439 Kelley Drive
West Berlin, NJ 08091
cs@townsendpress.com

ISBN-13: 978-1-59194-108-8
ISBN-10: 1-59194-108-3

Library of Congress Control Number:
2007910368

CONTENTS

ACKNOWLEDGMENTS

I could not have written this second book without the love and support of several people. To paraphrase an African proverb, it took a village to get this project to completion. There is not enough space to name all those involved, but I am confident that even without written acknowledgement, all those who shared in this project will celebrate with me and take pride in my accomplishments.

Thank you to Debra White for her editing skills and technical advice. Dan Harrison also provided editing and valuable input. Margaret Wilder, my good friend, provided not only inspiration but motivation to keep going. So did David Pijawka, another friend. I also thank the Godby family who gave me a second chance when I was a teenager in foster care many years ago.

Thank you to Beth Johnson, my editor who also became my friend, who believed in me at a time when it seemed no one else did.

And thank you to Dharma, my dog, for always sticking with me.

Thank you all for making another dream come true.

PROLOGUE

The weather was warm for early March in Tempe, Arizona, and I was drenched in sweat despite the air conditioning in my office. I was awaiting the outcome of a crucial meeting about my future as a professor at Arizona State University. The meeting would decide if I would be granted tenure—a permanent place on the faculty. Years of teaching, research, and writing had led up to this day. My perspiration was a result of nerves as much as the sweltering heat. Despite the three college degrees I earned, inside I still felt like a shy foster child, a little girl dressed in mismatched, hand-me-down clothing.

Today, a committee of my peers would review my educational path and pick apart my academic career. They would decide if I was good enough to earn tenure. As I waited for their judgment, I wondered, whatever they said, if *I* would ever think I was good enough. I wanted the affirmation of being the only African American ever tenured in ASU's College of Design. But even if I received that, would I still be the undeserving orphan I always felt I was? Could the kid with the too-dark skin, the one who could not read until the fifth grade, who never had a homemade birthday cake and never knew a family's unconditional love, ever feel good enough?

The news came in. I became the first African American, man or woman, to be tenured in the College of Design at Arizona State University. When my heart stopped pounding loudly in my ears, I managed to call my best friend Margaret Wilder with the news. Later that evening, I went out with friends to celebrate over Chinese food.

I felt happy and relieved. But hand in hand with that happiness came a sense of loneliness. Suddenly, I was thrust into serving as a role model for those who would come after me. Unless I achieved a string of successes, my critics would allege that other minority faculty members were not deserving of tenure. A heavy burden rested on my back. I had a lot to prove, not just for myself but also for other African American scholars. They depended on me to succeed.

Why me? How could I be anyone's role model? I was such an oddball. My faculty office resembled a monk's cell with bare walls. The shelves held few books. The walls were painted a drab color. The only sign of personality was an animal shelter calendar that featured photos of adopted dogs and cats. My office looked suited for a visiting professor, not someone who was a full-time faculty member. My home was similarly bare. I lived on the surface, never sinking down roots. Although years had past since I had left foster care, the system had left its marks on me. If I set down roots, someone might take away my happiness. So I lived as if I was packed and ready to move on a moment's notice. Would the timid little girl ever find her place in the world?

Like so many people who spent their childhoods as wards of the state, I felt undeserving. I belonged to no one but the system, and the system cannot give comfort to a love-starved child. A lifetime of rejection, and the defenses I threw up in response, prevented me from becoming whole. I grew up in bits and pieces, like a jigsaw puzzle. I might look whole on the surface, but I often felt shattered inside. A deep well of loneliness lingered in spite of later achievements.

Years of psychotherapy helped give me the skills to heal my soul. Beyond that, my greatest aide to healing has been putting my own story into words. In my first book, *Foster Care Odyssey: A Black Girl's Story*, I told of my experience growing up in foster care. The book you are holding picks up where that one ends.

To tell a balanced story, some people and incidents have been left out. I cannot remember the names of everyone involved. Records were not always available. I have lost touch with most people from my past. Much of the story, therefore, is recreated from memory. Names have been changed, but locations have not. The details may be hazy at points, but this is the life I lived beyond foster care.

CHAPTER 1

A College Career

In my first book, *Foster Care Odyssey: A Black Girl's Story*, I told how Catholic Charities dominated my childhood. The organization decided with whom I lived, for how long I stayed, and where I went to school. Foster care provided for my basic needs—food, shelter, and clothing—but it did nothing to prepare me for life on my own. If I had not run away from foster care when I was in high school, the system would have cut me loose when I graduated. As it was, at the tender age of 19 all I had was a high school diploma, a ragged suitcase with a few sets of worn clothes, and a burning ambition to prove I was somebody. As for marketable skills, I ran on near empty. If I was lucky, I might have passed a typing test at 25 words per minute. I was not a singer, dancer, or athlete. Nobody was knocking on my door with a job offer. A career as a cook or a maid had about the same appeal as boiled cabbage for breakfast: both made me sick. To avoid a life of panhandling or living in squalor, I hesitantly applied to college. Without family to lean on, I had no choice but to prepare myself for the future, wherever that might lead me.

At that time, 1973, blacks remained largely unwelcome in corporate boardrooms; television and movie roles portrayed us mostly as thugs or hookers. Regardless of the gains made by the civil rights movement, society remained largely segregated, and blacks had to work harder to press forward. I assumed this would be the same for me.

To say I was ready for college life would be a lie. On one hand, I threw my hands up in relief that I was no longer considered a "ward of the state." Whoever coined that term may have meant no harm, but I despised it. It made me feel like second-rate property and not a person. On the other hand, being separated from Catholic Charities terrified me. For years, the system took care of me. I did not have to think. I did not make decisions. They did it all for me. Now, they no longer wanted any part of me, whether I was ready to deal with the outside world or not. When prison inmates complete their sentences, they at least receive a small amount of money, bus fare, and maybe something decent to wear. Foster children receive nothing.

In June 1973, I sold my most valuable items, which amounted to a used guitar, a Timex watch that did not keep good time, and a pair of thinly lined winter boots. With the proceeds I bought a one-way ticket from my hometown—Buffalo, New York—to Boston. I had plans to attend a special summer program at Boston College, where I had been accepted on a four-year scholarship.

Jeanne O'Rourke, my friend and mentor who had been instrumental in my college-application process, drove me to the seedy bus terminal in downtown Buffalo. The surrounding neighborhood, once a vibrant transportation center where steady streams of blacks and other hopeful immigrants arrived looking for work, had sunk into decline when factories closed and jobs shifted to countries with cheaper labor and fewer government restrictions. Decay slowly eroded the once proud blue-collar city.

Because my bus was not scheduled to leave for another half-hour, Jeanne and I retreated to a small donut shop. Unemployed men with vacant stares sat huddled over dingy coffee cups. The smoke-filled air made my head feel like exploding. Jeanne glanced at my unhappy face and said, "How about breakfast?"

I shook my head "no."

"Are you sure?"

I gave her a weak smile. "Yes, I'm sure."

"It's a long ride. Can I convince you to have something? A donut or muffin, maybe?"

"I brought along turkey on a hard roll. I'll be fine."

"Do you mind if I eat?" Jeanne asked. "I haven't had breakfast yet."

For the next 15 minutes, I sat sandwiched in between Jeanne and an unemployed middle-aged man studying a thin column of want ads. Like me, Jeanne turned aside from the man's beaten-down face.

"This is a big day. Are you excited?" Jeanne asked.

My voice mirrored my feelings. Both were as bland as a plain white blouse. "No, not really."

"Jeez, I remember how I felt when I went off to college. I was a nervous wreck."

"No, I'm OK. Honestly." How could I tell her I was scared stiff?

"I'm glad you're taking this so calmly." Once she wiped her mouth with a napkin, she gave me a warm smile, the kind I could never muster. "Knowing you has enriched me."

"Thanks." By this time, she had to know most of our conversation would be terse. I doubted she expected any other response.

"Best of luck," Jeanne said, tenderly squeezing my hand. "I'll be expecting progress reports."

"OK."

Failure was not an option. If I dropped out, then what would I do? Spend my life as a beggar? I did not think I could handle the rigors of the military or solitude of the convent. College was all I had left.

Just then, an announcement crackled over the loudspeaker. My bus was boarding. We rushed through the terminal until we reached my gate. When Jeanne looked at me with teary eyes, I assumed she wanted a hug. I forced a smile, hoping that would satisfy her. It did not. She reached out and embraced me anyway. "Promise you'll call if you have problems."

"Sure." I doubted that I would.

Although I found it difficult to show my emotions, I did appreciate the help Jeanne gave me. She was a bright spot in my otherwise dark life. Without her, I might have drifted into a life of drugs and alcohol abuse. As I picked up my bag and headed for the bus, Jeanne unexpectedly followed me.

"Theresa, wait. I have something for you." I did not expect a gift; she had already gone out of her way by paying my college application fees. I was speechless when she handed me $100, which in 1973 was a tidy sum, especially considering she earned a modest salary as a counselor in a group home.

"Thank you." I slipped the cash inside my back pocket, waved good-bye and handed my ticket to the driver. In an instant, the bus pulled out of the terminal and I was on my way to an uncertain future.

As the Greyhound bus rumbled east along Interstate 90, the sight of the rolling hills and verdant scenery failed to hold my attention. I brought a copy of a *Time* magazine, but as I flipped the pages, words about the space station Skylab looked like gibberish. Sleep was impossible. I almost chewed my nails off. What would college be like? Would I pass? Would I get along with my classmates? Would people expect me to socialize? I was edgy about living in a city considerably larger than Buffalo, the only home I had ever known. Buffalo had not been a good home, but it was home nonetheless. By the time I arrived in Boston, I had probably dropped a pound from sweating so much.

Known locally as BC, Boston College is a private Jesuit institution situated along Commonwealth Avenue in Chestnut Hill, a separate city adjacent to Boston. Back then, BC sponsored the "Black Talent Summer Program" for minority students. The program helped underprepared students master the rigors of college. Its special curriculum reached out to high school students like me who not only lacked self-confidence but also carried the burden of inferior grades. The turbulent 1960s had brought calls for equality, with minorities demanding greater access to college campuses. Before that, most blacks were welcome only at historically black colleges. A few slipped into mainstream universities from time to time, yet most campuses shut their doors to us. To recruit minority students, several national initiatives were born. The program at BC was an offshoot of this movement. Other students who had already passed through the program played a major part in its operation.

Even though I am black and had lived in black foster homes, this was my first experience among virtually all black students. The Catholic schools I attended were predominantly white. Their modest tuition was beyond the reach of most blacks. Skin color did not separate me from the other summer students at BC, but religion certainly did. Most

blacks were of the Baptist faith. Hardly any identified with the Catholic Church, viewing priests and
nuns as hokey. Some even blamed the church for
not embracing a stronger stance against the evils
of Jim Crow, the discriminatory laws that had
oppressed blacks for so long. When those debates
came up I kept silent because the Catholic Church
was the only religion I had ever known. The Baptist
faith was alien to me.

Family situation also shoved an additional
wedge between us. Most of my fellow students were
reared in closely connected families, a tradition
we developed during slavery times. These young
people enjoyed the solid support of parents, aunts,
uncles, grandparents, cousins, and close family
friends. But no one except Jeanne and a few high
school classmates even knew I was in college.

Casting these differences aside, we had this in
common: we all felt compelled to achieve. College
was our ticket out of the ghetto. A lot of students
were the first in their families to attend college, and
they arrived with high aspirations.

I grew up to be an eccentric, never belonging
anywhere. I was at BC mostly because Jeanne had
insisted I apply. After all she did for me, how could
I let her down? Yet I was not sure this was the place
for me. Then again, was there any place for me? I
felt more out of place than the only black resident
in an all-white neighborhood.

I was socially awkward, with communication
skills that barely existed. I did not know how to
approach people, even those who I thought I would

like. Moreover, I was as plain as dry toast, not much different from the nuns I once lived with. I lacked with-it clothes, hip lingo, and the latest hairstyle. I had spent my life feeling excluded and I suspected the same thing would happen at BC.

Social situations were agonizing to me. I always looked for ways to avoid human interaction. That was how I lived as a foster child, without significant human contact. Hugs and kisses were as rare in my foster homes as reading and playing games. By the time I was a toddler, I had already been molded into a hermit. Whenever I had to interact with others in school, I fretted. That behavior pattern extended to adulthood. Now, I worried about college. I was hopeful that I could handle the academic requirements, but far from convinced I could deal with the social interaction. I found out how hard that would be during the first few days at BC.

On a break at an orientation session, a student name Carol approached me and asked, "Hey girl, where're you from?"

"Buffalo."

Carol ignored my brevity and easily shared her background. "I'm from D.C. I got six kids in my family. Two sisters and three brothers."

"That's nice." I wondered if my discomfort was obvious.

"Mom raised us because Daddy got hit by a car. How big is your family?"

"I don't have family." Carol looked at me like I had whipped out a pair of rosary beads, bowed my head, and started to pray. She seemed so unprepared for my response I felt sorry for her. I followed with my standard reply. "I was raised in foster homes."

The ends of Carol's lips curled downwards. All she could utter was an awkward "Oh."

Chatter about loving families heightened my awareness of what I missed and the growing void I felt. I refused to admit I still longed for something I would probably never have. Deprivation had started robbing my soul not long after birth. It never stopped.

I changed the subject and Carol never asked me another probing question. In fact, she avoided me. I kept my distance as well.

In time, though, a senior student wearing a nametag that identified her as Janet Freeman noticed I was always alone. Janet attempted to draw me into the group, but I resisted.

One day, however, Janet approached me. "What're you doing here all by yourself?"

From the corner of my eye, I noticed Carol still running her mouth. I felt envious because she seemed so at ease.

"I'm not good around groups," I said.

Janet tugged on my elbow and grinned. "Talk to me then. Let's find another seat."

"I . . . I . . ."

"Give me five minutes."

I acquiesced and followed her to an empty table.

For the next ten minutes, I reluctantly shared a little bit about myself. I surprised myself how quickly I relaxed around Janet. Perhaps our dark skin drew us together. Gentle in manners, but strong and proud, Janet was also very capable intellectually. She took no pity on me and treated me like any other student.

With an upbeat attitude, she said, "Not too long ago, none of us would be in college."

"I know."

"Some teachers and students will make hurtful remarks, but hold your head high. Don't get caught up in nonsense." In a sly manner, she lifted one eyebrow and said, "Get what I mean?"

"I think so, but I don't know if I can do the work. I always struggled in high school. What if I don't make it? I'm afraid of ending up as nobody doing nothing."

In grammar school, a series of standardized tests proved I was not retarded, as one of the nuns had insisted. The results showed that I had above-average intelligence, but that I was hampered by a learning disability. In fact, I was dyslexic. But I didn't get any help for my condition. Back then, disabilities drew scant attention unless they were obvious disorders like Down's syndrome or autism. Sometimes, I felt like the village idiot, even though test results showed otherwise.

"Girl, our people struggled for a *looong* time. College will be no different," Janet said. "You can make it here."

"You think so?" I did not see how I would.

"Believe in yourself. If you don't, who will?" She noticed the crowds were breaking up. "Remember,

I'll be there for you as much as I can."

For several hours a day that summer, I sat through college-level classes in economics, English composition, and social sciences. These were followed by a lengthy study period supervised by older students. The goal was to hone our skills so we could compete with white students. Although the civil rights movement had opened up doors for us, it had also brought about other, unintended changes. "White flight," the kind I had witnessed in Buffalo, had affected the entire public school system. Many white families had left the inner cities for the suburbs. Rather than allow their children to sit in the same classroom with minority students, the white families who stayed behind often enrolled their children in private schools. The loss of so many middle-class people deprived the public schools of a solid tax base for education. Minority children like me, educated in crowded, underfunded public schools, could not compete with white students taught in schools with more teachers, smaller class sizes, and ample resources. The program at BC was meant to put us on more equal footing.

Class work aside, I found dorm life to be a different kind of adjustment. College students went crazy away from home for the first time. Parties became a way of life. Unwanted pregnancies happened. Studying took a back seat. None of these temptations applied to me. I was untouchable.

Dormitory life nearly killed me. As a foster

child, I almost always had my own room, even if it was the size of a broom closet. But at BC, our rooms were like box-shaped walk-in closets with tiny shared bathrooms. Each suite had a living room for television viewing, radio listening, or hanging out. To reach my room, I had to pass through the living room. Whenever I did, there were always a handful of young women there. Men were not supposed to be there, but sometimes that rule was ignored.

My suitemates always said hello and asked me to join them. I shut them out at every turn. I expected them to start to hate me, but that did not happen.

Friendly and soft-hearted, my roommate Ruth wiggled her way into my life. One afternoon, I found her glued to Richard Wright's *Black Boy.* As I unloaded my backpack, she closed the book and said, "Hey girl, sit down and let's rap."

"I can't." I pointed to a pile of dirty clothes and said, "The machines are empty now, and I am almost out of clean clothes."

"The heck with the clothes," Ruth said. "Do not be one of them stuck-up bitches; just sit down. You're not in trouble or something?"

For the next half-hour or so, Ruth and I made a slight connection. When it came to emotions I always threw up roadblocks. Dying patients often isolate themselves. Feeling so alienated from ordinary life, I did the same. I was not about to drop my guard for Ruth. I did, nonetheless, crack open the door an inch or so. Whether she knew it or not, Ruth's persistence slightly eased me out of my detachment. Not much, but a little.

I finished my brief account of my life. Ruth sat silently for a moment.

"I don't know what to say," she finally said.

"There isn't anything you can say."

"I'm sorry, girl." She grasped my hand, but I held back. Ruth seemed to understand.

From that point on, Ruth took me under her wing. To avoid offending her, I went along. She introduced me to her circle of friends. Once in a while, I shared meals with her and other students who came from ghetto sections of big northeastern cities like New York, Baltimore, and Philadelphia. I picked up tidbits about popular black neighborhoods like Harlem and North Philly. As much as I enjoyed the company of these women, I was like a permanently disconnected phone line. It was still so hard to reach me. I was not sure I could end my years of self-imposed isolation. Then again, would I always live my life swallowed up in grief?

Themes of black power and ethnic pride resounded through the early 1970s. Large Afros and colorful dashikis were popular. Angela Davis was admired by some and feared by others. Eldridge Cleaver's book, *Soul on Ice,* was popular. Through aggressive and questionable tactics, the FBI picked apart the Black Panthers, but to many of us, the Panthers would always be winners.

I was surrounded by street savvy, which I lacked.

Conversations were peppered with street language that was as foreign to me as Greek. Fashion trends such as bell-bottoms, platform shoes, large hoop earrings, and polyester blouses with large collars that stretched to the shoulder were in vogue.

Some students in our program carried grudges against other black students and referred to them as "bitches." White people, mostly men, were either called "honkies" or "the man." My sheltered life in Buffalo did nothing to prepare me for life in the big city.

Early on that summer I was accused of conspiracy. One woman with an in-your-face attitude confronted me in the hallway and said, "I've seen you eating lunch too many times with *them*." She was referring to white people.

"I didn't know I was being watched," I said. "What do you mean?"

"We not black enough for you? Don't act so high and mighty, Miss know-it-all. You know exactly what I mean." She tossed her head back and sneered. "Talking like you're one of them on top of it."

I stood my ground. "Proper English is good for everyone. Ghetto language only stereotypes us as imbeciles. I'm here for an education, so I can get a job."

Such thoughtless comments shattered my confidence. I had always assumed that speaking standard English without ghetto slang would improve my lot in life. I had never regretted being born black. I was not material for any radical party, but I was proud of my heritage.

One night Ruth and a few sisters barged into my room and announced, "If you don't get dressed, we'll dress you and take you with us."

"No, really, I can't go."

When I saw Ruth and the others open my closet door and sort through my clothes, I gave in. "OK, I'll be ready in ten minutes!"

"Make it 5." Ruth winked and said, "I don't trust you."

Not surprisingly, the nightlife scene was largely segregated. Dance clubs for blacks, oddly enough, were not located in the black ghetto of Roxbury. Instead, they were squeezed into the downtown area near Boylston Street.

I was as graceless on the dance floor as someone on stilts. Disco was beginning to be popular. The song "Keep on Truckin'" by Eddie Kendricks was popular that summer, and it blared in the nightclubs we patronized. Young men tried to teach me a few steps, but I am one black woman not blessed with natural rhythm. The "Soul Train" chugged out of the station without me.

Narcotics were common on campus, but on our group outings, no one suggested getting high. As blacks in a primarily white city, we had to stay one step ahead of our white peers. If we got nabbed with drugs, we knew our punishment would be harsher than sentences meted out to whites. We kept clean because interaction with the police was tantamount to suicide.

As the summer went on, Ruth became fondly

critical of my wardrobe, made up of hand-me-downs and sale items. She insisted on taking me shopping in a popular commercial area called Downtown Crossing. "You need some snazzy clothes," she said bluntly. "You dress like an old maid."

How could I disagree? But I didn't have a clue what to do about it. And I was, as usual, broke.

"Girl, haven't you ever heard of Filene's Basement?" Ruth said with a huge grin. "It's the greatest place to shop in Boston."

"What is it?"

"What is it? A huge bargain basement that's got everything," Ruth said. "We'll find you some clothes that'll give you a lift."

"Do I really look that bad?"

"If I say yes, promise you won't be mad."

Filene's Basement was the most uncivilized department store in Boston. The place hopped with impatient, cost-conscious shoppers who snatched garments right out of other shoppers' hands. People pushed and shoved their way through the aisles, making me feel frantic. Since Filene's Basement had no dressing rooms, women whipped off their clothes and tried on new outfits on the spot, regardless of who surrounded them. An extremely modest person, I resorted to a more cautious way to see if something fit. Whenever I found an outfit I liked, I held it up against me. If it did not look like it would fit, I tossed it back into the bins and kept looking.

I prevailed through an exhausting afternoon. By the time we walked out, I had purchased two new outfits, which, according to Ruth, did not make me look like I was dressed for the Middle Ages. I vowed, however, to avoid Filene's Basement forever.

I shared a dorm room with three students. Generally, we tolerated one another, but tensions arose at night. Stella, a student from Baltimore, snored so loudly she sounded like the underground subway clanging through a tunnel. Needless to say, the rest of us missed out on a full night's sleep. At the end of four almost sleepless nights, we had a heart-to-heart talk with the offender, but Stella took the defense. She scrunched up her nose and said, "I can't help it, y'all."

"None of us can sleep listening to your big mouth. You ever hear yourself?" Ruth asked. "Girl, you sound like a rhino at a drag race."

"I'm not that loud," Stella insisted. "What you want me to do?"

Ruth glanced at the rest of us and said, "There's three other sisters here who can't sleep because of you."

"Y'all acting like I'm doing this on purpose."

Ruth shot back, "Get your noisy nose to cooperate and we'll all be happy."

The snoring dragged on and so did our restless nights. My roommates and I woke up groggy almost every morning. Sitting through class on four to five hours of sleep caused me to nod off now and then. To prevent mayhem, one of the program managers moved Stella to a private room. I heard her snoring was so noisy that students in the next room threatened to throw her off the John Hancock Tower if the noise persisted.

Janet Freeman, the senior student who had befriended me earlier, treated me like a younger sister. She checked up on me at least once a week. Usually we ate lunch in the dorm cafeteria. In spite of my interpersonal clumsiness, I felt a connection with Janet I did not enjoy with the others. We shared a few traits but differed in many ways. Reserved like me, Janet was mature for a 22-year-old college student. She seemed so worldly. She also had a polished elegance I longed to have. Underneath my emotional armor, I appreciated the way she cared about me. A huge chunk of me regretted I could not voice my thanks, and I trusted Janet understood.

I became more and more aware of how my past had crippled me. Constantly viewing myself as a boarder in someone else's home had hobbled my interpersonal skills. Every set of foster parents distinguished between foster children and their children. It was always us vs. them. All the foster families I lived with were poor, so they showered their children with praise and affection, if not gifts. I was ignored and never hugged. Research studies show that foster children often develop behavior problems. I could have told them that without any studies.

There were light-hearted moments over the summer. Streaking, also known as the art of running naked, prevailed on college campuses in the early 70s. One afternoon, Janet and I shared chicken salad sandwiches outdoors since the weather was so inviting. After lunch, we entered an elevator to take us to class when suddenly a white student jumped in, stark naked.

Janet looked coolly at the nude man and shook her head. She said, "Honey, cover up that puny pecker. I wouldn't flash that little bitty thing if I were you."

The man's face flushed as though it'd been burned by the Florida sun. He grabbed himself and dashed off the elevator, flapping away as he ran. Once he was out of sight, Janet and I looked at one another and fell out laughing. Janet heaved so hard her stomach ached.

Several weeks passed, and I slid into a predictable routine. Dorm life, however, was not so routine. Four women sharing a tiny bathroom created chaos, especially since everyone but me wore makeup. The proper application of eyeliner, eyebrow pencil, face powder, and lipstick took hours. Two of us wore large Afros, a hairstyle needing lots of time to pick and fluff to a good size. I forced myself out of bed at sunrise. The early hour allowed more than a 60-second shower and time to do my hair without another student banging on the door. For someone used to rules and order, the confusion grated on my nerves.

To get along with the others, I pushed my self into a compromise on some issues. As part of the bargain I made with myself, I rotated meal sharing. I sometimes ate with the black students, but once in a while I sat at a table with white kids I knew. Most often, I dined alone. Only one or two black students bugged me about eating with whites. Mostly, though, where or if I had meals became a non-issue.

Food was the typical institutional type. The canned vegetables were limp and salty. Fresh fruits were served on a haphazard basis. Dishes containing meat were often brackish, lacking any discernible taste. Servings of white bread and butter were plentiful. There was an endless supply of desserts, mostly glazed donuts, frozen layer cakes, and ice cream sandwiches. Because I was on the meal plan, I stuffed myself at every meal. In just a few weeks, my waistline expanded at least half an inch.

One evening, Ruth noticed I had passed through the food line twice. She stared at the slab of meat loaf on my plate, next to three pieces of bread and a hunk of cake. She asked, "Girl, how many people are you feeding?"

"Um . . . it's for me."

"If you keep on packing it away like that, you'll be a porker in no time."

My excessive eating had its roots in foster care. The families I lived with all survived on meager incomes, so usually there was not enough for second helpings. During particularly hard times, meals consisted of macaroni and cheese or canned mystery meat. Imagine my shock when the food at BC turned out to be abundant; I did not need permission to have seconds.

A Catholic school education had drummed a sense of order into my life. I was always on time and prepared for class. Some of my roommates, however, followed a tradition among certain blacks called "CP time" and breezed into class several minutes late. CP time stood for "colored people time," and it referred to tardiness, a common behavior in the ghetto. Obviously, the white professors weren't used to so many black students, let alone CP time. Several stern warnings about timeliness ended CP time that summer.

Although I reluctantly pushed myself to be sociable, I remained detached. Years of research have shown that children need adequate attachment relationships if they are going to develop normally. No kidding. I am a classic example of what happens when attachment relationships as an infant are fractured or non-existent. I have pored over research studies about maternal deprivation during infancy. I am not an expert in this field, but it is clear that nothing substitutes for a steady, nurturing figure, whether it is a man or a woman. I had neither. Sometimes I felt as if my feelings were permanently on ice.

If Prozac was around when I started college, I would have been the perfect candidate for this modern miracle drug. But the last thing I wanted was to immerse myself in the system again by asking to see a counselor. Janet Freeman was available, but I remained stoical and handled my problems alone, like I always had.

Books tucked underneath my arm, I left my room one evening and headed for the library. On the way, I bumped into Ruth. She tilted her head to the side and asked, "Girl, where're you off to?"

"The library."

"Want to come and chill out with a group of sisters?"

"No, I better not," I said. "I have this assignment due."

Ruth said, "Girl, you're such a party pooper. If you come to your senses, you know where to find us. Later for you girl."

Walking away, I wondered if I would always be such a bump on a log. Congenial women like Ruth attracted hordes of attention, yet I could barely say hello to people. Everyone in the program, it seemed, knew Ruth. How many people knew my name?

CHAPTER 2

A Girl Grows Up in Boston

Commonwealth Avenue was the main thoroughfare around BC and almost everyone referred to it
as "Comm Ave." Busses and the Green Line trolley
ran along Comm Ave. Since I did not have a car, I
relied on the extensive network of public transportation in and around Boston.

The surrounding area was dotted with handsome brick apartment buildings and majestic single-
family homes set on lush manicured lawns. There
were no visibly poor people around the predominantly upper-class Irish Catholic neighborhood.
Streets were free of litter and lined with elegant
elm trees that in autumn boasted gorgeous yellow,
orange, and red leaves. Although the neighborhood
was home to a popular university it was essentially calm and sedate, except on weekends during

football season, when throngs of avid fans flocked to BC for games. Chestnut Hill lacked the rat-race qualities common in other parts of the city.

One afternoon, as I ate lunch with Janet, I talked eagerly about my plans to explore the neighborhood. I viewed this as a constructive way to pass my time. Moreover, Boston was the first urban center I had visited. What I saw seemed so vastly different from Buffalo.

"I want to check out the area," I said. Walking alone relaxed me as well.

Janet frowned. "Be careful. People around here aren't used to chocolate faces."

"Are you saying I shouldn't go?"

"Don't go out at night, that's for sure." Janet tapped her fingers against the table and said, "Times have changed, but not that much."

I took Janet's sage advice to heart, yet my strolls turned out to be uneventful. I followed the same route almost daily. A few neighbors eyed me suspiciously at first, but once they saw my face over and over, they grew more comfortable in my presence. Occasionally, I received a friendly nod. One woman even greeted me as I passed by her graceful red brick home late in the afternoon. No one ever invited me in for lemonade, but I was not hassled either.

Those long walks temporarily relieved my concern about living in close quarters with young women who were miles away from me. Intellectually we were on the same level, but emotionally I lagged years behind. They were slick, street-wise sisters, while I was like a country bumpkin from the back-waters.

Part of me grew envious of classmates with doting boyfriends. I was happy my sisters shared the company of thoughtful black men, but seeing them together made me feel lonelier than ever. Would I ever be in the same position, or forever immersed in solitude? I had a hard enough time relating to other women. Talking to men was out of the question. Missing from my teenage years were the usual rites of passage—crushes on boys, holding hands at the movies or kissing at the school dance. I feared I would be a lonely old biddy for the rest of my life.

Ruth's boyfriend showered her with gifts, such as the latest disco records, gold earrings, and chocolate candy. Every so often, he popped up in the dorm with a bouquet of fresh daisies. He could not afford roses. The only gifts I'd ever received were during the holiday season, when local charities distributed donated goods to foster children. Was I unappreciative of the good deeds of strangers? Perhaps so, but I wanted to be someone's angel. Instead, I lugged around feelings of worthlessness. Wallowing in self-pity would drag me further into a bottomless pit, so I tried to keep up a fake front and show people I was interested in life. But really I was not.

Throughout the summer, I exchanged several letters and postcards with my friend Jeanne from

Buffalo. Numerous studies indicate that foster children usually have at least one strong relationship in their lives. We seek outside friendships because we have no family. For me that strong relationship was Jeanne O'Rourke.

In her latest missive, she surprised me by saying she wanted to visit Boston. I wrote back and told her I welcomed her company. I never thought she would come.

As I was holed up in my room cramming for an exam, one of my dormmates knocked on the door. There was a call for me on the pay phone in the hallway. It was Jeanne.

The sound of her voice whisked me back to my dismal days in Buffalo. As hard as I tried to distance myself from the emotional torment I left behind, talking to Jeanne linked me to a past I could not escape. I wondered if I ever could. I stumbled as I tried to speak. Once I composed myself, I filled her in on my progress thus far, how I fared in college classes and my adjustment to dormitory living. She listened intently to everything I said, including what were probably boring details about the Boston subway system and the architectural style of the homes in Chestnut Hill.

At the end of our conversation, there was a pause. Then she said, "So, what about a visit soon?"

From time to time, other students received visits from family members, friends, or lovers. For a change, I would have a visitor. I threw some ice on my feelings so she would not think I was lonely, but she probably knew anyway. "That'd be nice, but I don't think you can stay in the dorm."

"I'll find a place to stay."

"You sure?"

"Yes, I'm sure. And keep up the good work."

She had more faith in me than I did. "Thanks, I'll try."

"I look forward to my trip."

So did I.

Despite being enrolled at a Jesuit college, some students had active sex lives, including Ruth. What she did in her private life was none of my business, but when she used our room for intimacy without warning me I was affected.

Late one afternoon, I returned to our dorm suite, exhausted from a day of lectures. Books in my arms, I juggled my keys to open the lock. I thought I heard grunts and groans, but brushed them aside as daytime drama from the TV room. Opening the door, I flipped on the lights, then stopped dead in my tracks. Quite unwittingly, I had interrupted Ruth and her boyfriend in the height of passion.

Ruth wrapped a bed sheet over her naked body while her boyfriend Jamal grabbed his pants and ducked into the closet.

"I'm sorry," I said, not sure what to do or say. To avoid Ruth, I bent down to pick up the books I had dropped on the floor. Once I gathered my things I hesitated to stand up. Eventually I did, only to find Ruth scrounging for clothes.

Blouse half-buttoned and her Afro flattened and out of shape, Ruth zipped her blue jeans and shrieked. "Oh girl, that hurt."

"What's the matter?" I asked.

"I snagged my damn hair!"

An awkward moment of silence passed, then we both cracked up.

"I had no idea you were here," I said, with a slight grin.

"I should've told you, but I thought you'd be gone all afternoon."

Then we heard a loud thump from the closet.

"Oh my God. Jamal is still hiding," Ruth said as she laughed even harder. "Give us a few minutes, and then we'll be gone."

As I walked out the door, I said, "I'll wait in the community room."

"You won't tell anyone, will you?" Ruth asked.

"Not a soul."

Although I was curious about sex, I had not yet crossed that line. Sex was very private, not something I viewed as casual. I was also apprehensive about letting myself go with men who I barely knew. I didn't want to come across as a prude, but undoubtedly I did. I felt so awkward about dating that I avoided it altogether.

Information about birth control on campus was as rare as blacks in South Boston. The senior students in charge, however, realized the dangers of unprotected sex, so they supplied students with condoms and what information they could. BC's medical department did not dispense birth control, as doing so would be against Catholic policy. Condoms were not foolproof, and unwanted pregnancies sometimes happened.

Early one morning, Ruth beat me to the shower. To keep my place, I waited outside the door. As I mulled over my schedule for the day, I heard Ruth heave in the bathroom. Just what I needed, I thought, to catch a stomach virus when I had a term paper due.

Back in our room, Ruth was queasy again. She flopped onto the bed, pressing a wet cloth against her face.

"What's wrong?" I asked. I had not yet caught on.

"Morning sickness," she said, wiping perspiration from her brow. "I think I might be sick again."

"I heard the flu is going around campus." I still was in the dark.

"Girl, I'm not sick, I'm pregnant," Ruth said.

"Pregnant!" I said.

"Lord have mercy, don't broadcast it to the whole campus," Ruth said, motioning me to be quiet. "No one else knows."

"What will you do?"

"I've talked it over with Jamal, and he'll pay for an abortion," she said. "We can't drop out of college. We worked too hard to get here."

Ruth needed a hug, but that I could not do, so I said, "I'm not here to judge. I respect whatever choice you make."

"Adoption isn't an option," Ruth said, voice cracking. "No way am I giving my baby to strangers. This is the best Jamal and I can do."

With few exceptions, black students on campus banded together. True, there was nothing like the physical violence that at one time had pervaded the South, but the lives of black and white students were largely separated.

Laurie, a young woman from New York City who lived in my suite, surprised us one weekend when she entertained company.

"Hey everyone, meet my family," Laurie said, nodding towards a middle-aged white couple and two teenaged girls with red hair and freckles.

We had known that Laurie, an only child, had lost her parents in a house fire while she was at school. Her neighbors quickly gave her a new home. None of us, however, knew those neighbors were white.

Dottie, presumably the mom, extended a warm hello to a group of black women with mouths wide open. "It's nice to meet you all. Laurie has told me all about you."

A clumsy moment passed when Laurie glanced at a handsome man who looked like Sean Connery. "Our dads worked together and were good friends."

Ruth smiled and said to Laurie's family, "I hope you enjoy your visit to Boston."

"Same here," I said.

As soon as Laurie and her family left the room, a smart-mouthed student said, "I see girlfriend is spending the day with white bread."

Another street-savvy sister said, "Maybe we should remind her she's black."

Throughout that weekend, those two students launched swipes at Laurie's family, but I did not share their anger. I distanced myself from the snide comments because they were uncalled for. Laurie had a family. What did it matter if they were from a different race?

Laurie spent the weekend at the hotel where her family had rented a suite. When she returned, a few icy stares greeted her, but within several days students were more concerned about their own term papers and upcoming final exams than with the skin color of Laurie's family.

I should have opened up to Laurie about my own background, but my reclusive nature held me back. Most likely we could have become friends, but I shied away from revealing too much to a woman I still saw as a stranger. I regret not giving her the chance by remaining in my cocoon.

Since my roommates acted as if they were face-to-face with bank robbers when introduced to Laurie's family, I decided not to introduce Jeanne on her upcoming visit. How would they react to another white face so soon? In the troubling years of the 1970s, blacks often felt we had to be blacker than the next black person. It took a while before we appreciated being black as more than darker skin pigmentation or saying the right slogan. I viewed blackness as a shared ideology, involving caring for other black people.

I rode the trolley to meet Jeanne on the day she arrived. Her modest income led her to a drab motel on the edge of the red-light district. It was still afternoon, so I figured we would be safe from the pimps, drug addicts, and hookers who infested the area like roaches.

I was pleased yet nervous about seeing Jeanne again. She was the closest thing I had to family, yet we really were not that close, mostly because of me. As I asked the clerk in the shabby lobby for her room number, my mouth became as dry as the sand at Cape Cod. I gulped down water before getting on the elevator. But when she opened the door and smiled at me with those warm brown eyes, my anxiety quickly melted.

I sensed Jeanne would reach out to hug me, so I tried not to clam up the way I usually did. She threw her arms around me and said, "It's so good to see you."

I mustered a one-word reply and a tepid hug. "Likewise."

Gently holding my hand, she led me inside her sparsely furnished room. "Sit down and let's talk."

It felt as if we had been separated for ages, yet it had only been two months ago since I left Buffalo. Strangely, I was interested in local news, even though most of it was depressing. More factories had closed down, unemployment soared, and

Governor Rockefeller seemed out of touch with the cruel realities thrashing the state. Upstate New York still reeled from the bloody uprising at Attica State Prison, brutally crushed in 1971.

Over cheeseburgers and vanilla Cokes at a nearby greasy spoon diner, Jeanne made a startling revelation. "Theresa, I'm getting married."

She had been dating, but I had not known she was serious about her boyfriend. I said, "I'm glad for you. When's the big date?"

"We haven't set one yet, but I'm leaning towards next year. His family doesn't have much, and I can't expect them to pay everything. My father got laid off." She seemed embarrassed.

"I'm sorry."

"Dad was devastated. It's hard for a 58-year-old man without a high school education to find work. But let's not talk about me. I have a question for you."

What did she want? If I had money, I surely would have given it to her. "Sure, what's up?"

"Be in my wedding."

"Me? Really?"

"Yes, I'd like you to be one of my bridesmaids." She smiled and said, "What about it?"

"I'm honored. Yes, of course, I'll be in your wedding."

After Jeanne left, I was filled with anxiety. How could I, the social dud, endure the celebration associated with a family wedding? I was so honored that Jeanne wanted me, and later I learned that Ed, her fiancé, was enthusiastic about me participating as well. As it turned out, of course, I survived the experience, but it had its awkward moments. I could not pay for my bridesmaid's dress, and I felt ashamed to accept Jeanne and Ed's help. I agonized over my gangly, graceless appearance and spent hours practicing teetering along in high heels as I prepared for the big event. In the otherwise all-white bridal party, I felt like my black face stuck out outrageously. Once again, I realized dispiritedly, what should have been an easy, happy experience was made difficult and joyless because of my odd nature.

At the end of a grueling summer, I finally mastered my courses, including trigonometry, a subject that almost caused me to hurl my textbook into the Charles River. I was so delighted with my A and B grades I even attended a farewell party my roommates organized. And for a change, I danced the night away.

In bed the next morning, I ruminated about the past few months. The Black Talent Program did more than simply bring together a group of diverse young black men and women. Lasting friendships were nurtured. Some couples shared more than just a summer fling and made plans to stay together. Several would soon be parents. Like all people, we bickered from time to time. Stella, the roommate who snored, tested our nerves. The bathroom routine also caused a lot of frayed tempers. On the whole, though, we all matured a bit, becoming better prepared to handle the rigors of full-time college study.

By the time I was packed, all of my roommates had departed except for Ruth. I knew I would not be seeing her again. Jamal had joined the armed forces and was going overseas, and she was going to marry him and go along. For a second, my throat tightened as I glanced at Ruth. Once I regained composure, I walked her to the front door.

"Hey, good luck," she said.

"Yeah, you too."

"Was nice sharing a room with you."

"Same here," I said. "Thanks for looking out for me."

She was as warm as always. "You got my address. Let me hear from you."

"OK."

She drew back and studied me with quizzical eyes. "Why don't I believe you?"

"You'll hear from me. I promise."

Ruth threw her arms around me and held me close. For someone so disconnected as I was, the embrace felt good. "I know you won't, but don't forget me. Take care of yourself."

Predictably, I failed to keep in touch. That was not the time for me to end years of self-imposed isolation. I wondered when or if that time would ever come, or would I always feel ready for a funeral?

CHAPTER 3

My College Career Begins

Fall courses did not start for another week, so I welcomed a brief reprieve. A steady routine of class attendance and study had drained me both mentally and physically. My previous schools in Buffalo had made few demands on me. Grammar and high school teachers viewed black students as having less potential than our white counterparts, so they generally ignored us. It was normal when white students talked about their aspirations to become lawyers, physicians, and astronauts, but when black students voiced similar dreams, our hopes were always squashed.

I ran up against some BC professors who seemed to hold negative attitudes towards their black students. One summer-school professor chastised me and a few other black students for being lazy when we had trouble understanding complicated trigonometry concepts. Perhaps I failed to appreciate how or if the Pythagorean theorem would impact my future, but I stayed up late many nights trying to figure it out. In a fit of temper one morning, this tart-tongued professor, looking like he was sucking on a lemon, said, "All you people are the same. You just don't get it." Most of us sat there in stunned silence. One woman dabbed a tear on her cheek. This arrogant twit in a seersucker suit and blue silk bowtie clearly failed to appreciate we had come from crumbling schools with second-rate textbooks. Our mostly uninterested or inexperienced teachers lacked the expertise necessary to guide poor urban kids. As much as we wanted to compete on an equal footing with white students, the vestiges of poverty and racism rendered that nearly impossible.

During my week off, I enjoyed my usual rambles around the neighborhood, wondering if the scent of autumn sweetening the air would invigorate me. The early fall weather transformed green leaves into vibrant shades of orange, red, and yellow. Some days I felt as if I could walk forever —alone of course. As long as I avoided human contact, I felt safe.

Each day became an adventure because I discovered another part of Boston. Growing up in Buffalo did not prepare me for the crowds, but I managed. Particularly enthralling was Newberry Street, a major thoroughfare running right through well-to-do Back Bay, home to a pocket of upper-crust citizens. All I could do was window-shop; the stores along this trendy street sold high-priced goods far beyond my skimpy budget. I became acquainted with fashionable names such as Gucci and Bill Blass, brands unheard of during my childhood. If my foster mother Mrs. Woodson had seen me peeping in those stores, she would have raised hell. The payments she received from Catholic Charities were never enough, and she constantly fretted about making ends meet. Bargain brands and discards at second-hand stores dominated my wardrobe.

I rarely saw another black face along Newberry Street, except for men who swept streets or drove delivery trucks. Mistrust and fear were so widespread that shopkeepers automatically locked their front doors whenever they saw me peering through the window. Janet had warned me about this. When I told her I sometimes meandered down Newberry Street, her eyes opened so wide it looked as if she stepped on a live wire.

"You're likely to give some of those people a heart attack," she warned. "Or they'll call the police. Watch yourself."

"I don't worry," I said.

"You should."

Still, I remained undaunted. Even though I barely scraped up enough money for carfare and lunch, I ventured along Newberry Street every so often. Certainly, there was no way I could afford the prices, but I basked in extravagant fantasies where I wore stylish clothes and never glanced at the price tag.

On days when my feet failed to cooperate, I hopped on the train and rode all over Boston. One time I made the dreadful mistake of riding the train during rush hour. Crowds of weary, pushy downtown office workers on the way home almost flattened me as I jockeyed for space. I swore never again to use public transportation during rush hour.

Across the slowly meandering Charles River, I discovered the nearby city of Cambridge, home to Harvard and MIT. These two large, elite private colleges accepted only the brightest students. A feeling of anything goes prevailed in Cambridge. Boston felt stiffer, just like my emotional state.

Checking out Harvard Square late one afternoon, I heard a few people mention boating along the Charles River. I asked a man selling newspapers how to get to the river, and he pointed me in the right direction. As I approached, my attention was grabbed by the young people propelling sleek wooden boats up and down the murky river. From listening to other people's conversations, I learned these were "crew teams" and that intense rivalries existed among the rowers at Boston-area colleges. BC had a crew team. Skimming along the water looked like fun. For a moment I considered joining, but I doubted I was fit enough to make the team. I also thought my color would make a difference. There were not many blacks at BC, and rowing was not a sport popular in our communities. Some people lived near water, but could not afford boats.

Over the next semester, I regularly rode the Red Line to Harvard Square and made my way to the Charles. I was content to sit along the river's edge and watch boats full of healthy, muscular students as they practiced their sport, even in raw, nasty weather.

I enjoyed wandering around Harvard Square, the heart and soul of Cambridge, where street life was far more lively than anything I had seen in Buffalo. The mostly white crowds, all of whom I assumed were connected to either Harvard or MIT, intimidated me. No one ever threw a disparaging comment at me like, "What're you doing around here?" Nonetheless, I felt out of place. During my jaunts around "the square," as most local residents referred to it, I kept to myself and avoided conversation with other young people. I assumed they would not want to talk to me anyway, but I was wrong. The ranks of the 1960s flower children had thinned out considerably, but some stubbornly refused to let go of that laid-back era and wore tie-dyed shirts, tattered bell-bottom jeans, and flashed the ubiquitous peace sign. Racial harmony had been one of the keystones of the hippies; I'm confident now they would have been friendly and welcoming to me.

On a quiet stroll one morning through Chestnut Hill, thoughts about a group home where I had lived for a few years as an adolescent popped into my head. The home, Flourette Hall, had been operated by a small order of nuns called the Sisters of Good Hope. The order, I remembered, had its headquarters in Chestnut Hill. What should I do? Make a social call on them or store that experience in the back of my mind forever? It was not like I could call the nuns up and say, "How about meeting me for a jelly donut? Or do you want to catch a Celtics game at the Garden?" The minute I returned to campus, I made up my mind to call anyway.

Part of me was still angry with the Catholic Church for closing Flourette Hall. To the Church, it had become a financial burden, but to those of us who lived there, it was home. I was curious about some of the nuns who I lived with during those years, except for the nun who molested me. I hoped she had retired and was prevented from working with children. Beyond my curiosity, I also wanted the nuns to see I was in college. I wanted them to know I was not a loser who had fallen into society's black hole.

After breakfast the next morning, I dropped a dime into a pay phone in the dorm hallway and dialed their number. The phone rang only twice when a shaky voice said, "Good morning."

"Could I speak to Sister Petrina?"

"That's me. May I help you?"

I stuttered for a second then said, "My name is Theresa Cameron. Remember, from Flourette Hall in Buffalo? I'm in Boston now."

Sister Petrina answered in that patronizing, overly sweet tone that I thought of as peculiar to nuns. "Yes dear, I remember."

"I'm at Boston College."

The old nun perked up a bit, but she was also incredulous. "You're at BC?"

"I just started."

I was surprised when she said, "Please, come over and see me."

Half an hour later, I stood before a solid black wrought-iron gate. Behind it were three stately two-story brick homes. They looked like historic brownstones in parts of New York City. Security was lax, so I opened the gate and let myself in. The half-acre lawn and all the hedges were clipped short, giving the place the neatness of a Palm Beach golf resort. Window boxes filled with bright red geraniums rested in front of each first-story window. An elm tree with leaves the color of saffron and cantaloupe stood by the front gate. Inside the driveway sat a typical nun-mobile, a spotless, dull gray Buick station wagon. These nuns seemed to live well.

Differences abounded among Catholic nuns. The Sisters of Good Hope were a small but elite group who amassed a considerable amount of property. Each well-educated nun came from an Irish Catholic family with deep pockets. These women may have taken vows of poverty, but their living arrangements were very different from most Catholic nuns, who lived in austere environments in poverty-stricken neighborhoods or Third World countries.

A soft rap on the door brought me face-to-face with Sister Petrina. Liver spots covered her shaky hands. Wrinkles aged her face. Her gait seemed considerably slower than the days when she ran about yelling at us to wash the dishes or turn down the stereo. Always slender, Sister Petrina was even thinner.

The relaxed dress code that had resulted from an important Catholic conclave in the early 60s, known as Vatican II, had not affected these nuns. As always, Sister Petrina was clad in a head-to-toe black habit with a large strand of rosary beads draped around her waist.

"Please, come in."

She held open the door with its prominent crucifix attached, and I followed her inside a softly lit hallway. A Persian rug covered part of the shiny wooden floors and the ceilings were so high our voices bounced off the plain white walls.

Once inside, Sister Petrina carefully checked me out as if I was there for inspection. Her stare was intrusive, but then again, she was a quizzical one even when I knew her. She beckoned me to follow her into an elegant sitting room, where she gestured towards two empty high-backed oak chairs. No matter how ornately the home was decorated, it felt as cold as a long winter in Buffalo.

Sister Petrina smiled gently. "I like it when our girls keep in touch with us." I was now a woman, but I let it pass. She meant well. "How have you been?"

I omitted some of the more painful details about my ordeal since Flourette Hall had closed, such as running away to California, confinement in two juvenile-detention facilities, and a suicide attempt, but I told her I graduated from high school and was about to start college at BC.

"That's so nice, dear."

I considered opening up to her, thinking for a moment that she might understand how hard it had been to grow up on my own. But I abandoned that idea. Probably no one but another foster child could really comprehend. So I asked, "What goes on here?"

"We run a small orphanage." I was surprised a nun her age still worked. I thought she was ready for retirement when she was at the group home.

She explained that every nun was expected to participate, unless prevented by sickness, age, or dementia. Evidently, Sister Petrina was not old or feeble enough to escape child-care duties. She chuckled as she said, "I'm even learning how to deal with black children's hair."

"Want any help?"

"I think I've got it down now, but I used to have such a hard time." She stifled a laugh. "The clerks at the drug store used to stare at me when I bought Afro Sheen."

It was hard to hide my amusement at the thought of Sister Petrina buying black hair-care products.

"Would you like to visit the children?"

"Yes, I'd like that." I was surprised I said yes.

Twenty children, from 3 to 5, lived next door to the nun's residence. Of different races, these children were abandoned, disabled, abused, or neglected. Children not placed by the state sometimes ended up with the Sisters of Good Hope. Usually the arrangement was temporary, but Sister Petrina quietly acknowledged two of the children had lived with them since birth.

Sister Petrina seemed emotionally detached from the sad faces in front of her as she chatted on about changes in the Archdiocese of Boston and how hard it was to attract young women to the convent. I did not care if the bishop wanted a new car or nun recruitment had hit an all-time low. All I could do was stare at the needy young children reaching out for affection. Tears filled my eyes, but I refused to cry. I saw so much of myself in these children that I cut my visit short. Facing the past was more than I could handle.

I turned to Sister Petrina and told her a tiny fib. "It was very nice to see you again, but I have to get back to the dorm."

"Can't you stay for lunch? Our cook is making meat loaf today. If I remember, didn't you like meat loaf?"

"I have your number so I'll call. We can have lunch some other time."

She extended an unsteady hand. "I was hoping you'd stay a little longer and maybe help me out with the children. You'll come back, right?"

"Yes, I will." I doubted I would.

Sister Petrina gestured towards the door. "Let

me show you out. I'm sorry you have to leave."

The unhappy faces of those children stuck with me as I walked down the path. I made a decision that I would somehow, soon, break out of my isolation and find a place where I could offer solace to other needy children. Gradually, my feelings of sadness shifted to rage. I was angry that helpless children suffered because of parental ignorance and society's neglect. I was furious that I had needlessly endured much of the same.

Racial discrimination had compounded my situation. After my birth, for reasons I will never know, my mother turned me over to Catholic Charities. She failed to list my father's name on the birth certificate. That left no way to locate family members who might have been willing to assume my care. Parental rights should have been severed much sooner than the ten years it took New York State to do so. My birth mother's actions constituted abandonment because she did not visit me for six consecutive months—in fact, I never saw her again. Nor did she make plans for my future. Nearly 11 when I was legally freed for adoption, I then carried the label "hard to place." Older, black, and wedged at the bottom of the adoption list, I was not a hot commodity.

*   *   *

Boston College became more vibrant during the week between summer and fall semesters. Bewildered-looking freshmen arrived daily, as did returning students. I watched young men and women as they carried overstuffed suitcases along narrow campus pathways to their dorms. Friendships interrupted by summer vacation slowly rekindled. Although the turbulent protests of the 60s had withered away, new placards sprang up around campus denouncing President Nixon and the Vietnam War, in spite of a recently signed peace accord.

Alone in my room since my new roommate had yet to arrive, I opened a note from the office of student affairs. The young woman's name was Vanessa Hampton. Reading the note made my knees feel like jelly. I would have preferred a room to myself, but as a student on a scholarship, the luxury of a single room was not available.

I sat by the open window and peered at the social activity brewing below. The idea of mingling with new students made me so nervous I decided to escape until classes began. Foster care had taught me to be frugal, and I had stashed away some money. Now was the right time to spend it.

The next morning I threw some clothes into a small canvas bag. A gasoline crisis led me to the bus station instead of a rental-car office. With no particular place in mind or a map to guide me, I bought a ticket to Kittery, Maine. That was as good a choice as any, I thought.

Several hours later, I found myself on a vast stretch of shoreline in southern Maine. Having never seen the ocean as a child, I parked myself on a boardwalk bench. The awe-inspiring beauty of Maine's rugged coast, with pristine beaches and the sound of waves crashing onto shore, filled me with a sense of serenity, one I rarely experienced. Unlike the heavily polluted Charles River, the Maine waters looked fresh and clean. Summer was at an end so temperatures were nippy. A few cyclists cruised along the boardwalk, but no one braved the cold ocean water. Chilly breezes blew in from the Atlantic and the salty aroma tickled my nose. When winds kicked up in Buffalo, the only smell was rancid air from the smokestacks. In front of me, small boats bounced along choppy waters. On the horizon, I traced the outline of huge ocean liners as they sailed to distant ports. For the first time in my life, I felt an strong attraction to the sea. The immense Atlantic was filled with so many unknowns, much like my own life. Someday, I vowed, I would live by the ocean in a house as elegant as those in Chestnut Hill. I would no longer live on borrowed time.

The sun disappeared while I was lost in thought. As the only black person on a deserted beach in a primarily white community, I hurried off the unlit boardwalk. Maine was not Mississippi, but why take chances? I hoped my skin color would not deter me from finding a motel room, and fortunately, it did not. Now that the busy summer season had tapered off, I surmised either the innkeeper was glad for the business or my dark brown skin did not frighten him off.

I woke up feeling refreshed after a solid eight-hour sleep. Showered and dressed, I returned my room key and asked the manager to recommend a good place for breakfast. From my own experiences with racism and countless stories I had both heard and read, I expected a cold reception when I walked into the local diner, but there was nothing eventful as the baby-faced waitress asking me whether I wanted hot cakes or scrambled eggs. There were only a handful of customers.

The waitress handed me the check and said, "Where you headed?"

"I have a few days before school starts. I thought I'd see New England. Any suggestions?"

Lifting her shoulders slightly, the waitress replied, "Not much goes on now that summer is over. About the only attraction we have are the beaches."

"Maybe I'll take a ride up I-95 and check out another part of the state."

The waitress narrowed her eyes and said, "Don't go walking around on those country roads. Some truckers drive like maniacs. I know because I've lived in Maine my whole life."

I wondered if she was hinting that people might mistreat me. Once I paid my tab, I changed my mind and got on a bus headed for the White Mountains of New Hampshire. Little did I know the "Live Free or Die" state was extremely white as well as staunchly conservative. Mere mention of the word "tax" would start a revolt.

The bus got off the interstate, and my interest increased. As the driver cruised along sparsely traveled country roads, I was stunned by the stately homes we passed. Victorian houses fit for royalty sat on large pieces of perfectly landscaped property. There were knee-high walls made of stones running along the perimeter of each owner's property. Gravel-filled driveways seemed a mile long. Every now and then, the bus passed what were probably family-owned dairy farms, where small herds of cows nibbled on patches of grass. These magnificent sights were the opposite of the plain and sometimes dumpy neighborhoods I grew up in. Except for the exquisite private homes around Boston College, I had only seen houses like these in library books or the movies.

Face pressed against the window, I glanced at modest houses, small farms, and fall foliage. Already, leaves were turning shades of rust and pumpkin. Blue skies dappled with puffy clouds as white as snow made the lonely bus trip not quite so dreary. On a whim, I exited the bus in a small village south of the White Mountains. While munching on a snack, I felt sad because I had no one to share my adventure with. Other tourists traveled in pairs or in groups, and everyone, it seemed, had someone to talk to. Watching others interact heightened my solitude and instead of enjoying my journey, I felt crushed. I wanted to be with someone other than myself. No longer interested in exploring New Hampshire, I moseyed around until I found an inexpensive motel. I returned to Boston early in the morning, feeling anxious about meeting new students and studying full time. In spite of a successful summer-school session, I still was not sure I would make it beyond freshman year.

Campus had filled up considerably during my short absence. The school had appeared much larger over the summer because only a handful of students occupied its grounds. There were at least 10,000 students, faculty, and staff members at BC. The school had lost its small-town atmosphere and was more like a city within a city. Everything was so different from my sheltered life in Buffalo.

My impromptu trip to New England had served as a stall tactic. Once again, I broke into a sweat just thinking about my new roommates. By this time, I should have been accustomed to change, since I spent so much time moving around and living with strangers. Nonetheless, it never got any easier. I dreaded answering the inevitable family questions I was sure to be hit with.

Weaving my way among a multitude of unfamiliar faces, I made it back to my dorm. Before I left, I was the only resident. Every suite was now occupied, including mine. A wave of jitters bounced around in my stomach as I passed through the communal area, where five other young black women were engaged in a lively conversation about Watergate. Whatever illegal activities Richard Nixon and his colleagues had committed were of little concern to me, but Watergate grabbed most people's attention.

When I stopped in front of the women who I would spend the next year living with, we all looked at one another and laughed awkwardly. A petite woman with a large Afro and clear skin the color of mocha took the lead and spoke first. She met me with a disarming smile, introduced herself as Vanessa Hampton. She extended her tiny hand and said, "Hi, it's nice to meet you. Are you Theresa?"

I tried to smile pleasantly but felt strangled. I forced a grin and replied, "Likewise."

The rest of us introduced ourselves, and I relaxed a bit since no one asked me about my past. I expected at some point the questions would come, but at least it was not right off the bat.

With a snap of her fingers, Vanessa then said, "Listen up, everyone. It's good we're all here, so we can get to know one another."

We nodded agreement.

"Let's go out to eat," Vanessa said. "This way we can set ground rules, so we can live with one another."

When everyone grabbed the idea, I knew I should go along. Somehow, some way, I would have to work on shedding my shyness. Whether I liked it or not, group living would be part of my life for the near future. I doubted my new roommates would understand if I backed out of this first get-together. In order to graduate, I had to adjust to dorm life. I had nowhere else to live.

During a casual dinner of double-decker hamburgers, grilled-cheese sandwiches, and French fries laden with grease, we spent time getting to know one another. Agreeing on house rules would come later. Each woman talked about her family, friends, what life was like in her hometown, and what she wanted to major in at BC. Most importantly, though, we shared one common goal—to earn a college degree and a way out of poverty, a goal not possible for many of those who came before us.

By the time apple pie a la mode and mugs of hot coffee and tea were served, it was my turn. Oh, how I dreaded these moments. To hide my shaky hands, I stuck each flattened palm underneath my thighs. In my usual unflappable voice, I offered just enough to satisfy my new roommates. When I took a breather, everyone sat there and stared at me in disbelief. Vanessa went first and said, "Girl, you're for real, aren't you?"

The moment my eyes signaled the affirmative, she said, "I'm sorry."

A bit of sudden confidence made the next round of conversation a little easier. "Don't feel sorry for me. There were others who had it harder than me."

"Why didn't they try to find you a permanent home?" Vanessa said.

My voice lowered as I continued, "It's something I avoid talking about." This was not the time to engage in a debate about the shortcomings of the child-welfare system and the lack of political will to make changes.

Vanessa quickly glanced at the others and said, "Girl, you've got nothing to feel embarrassed about."

The other young women silently nodded. One reached out and squeezed my hand.

I picked up a napkin, wiped the sweat from my forehead, and said, "Let's talk about something else, OK?" Talking about my background rarely made me feel better, as a few therapists suggested it would. The unknown circumstances of my birth and the subsequent 19 years I spent as a ward of New York State refused to loosen their grip on me.

Around 10 p.m., we called it a day. We wandered along Comm Ave and finally reached campus. The clear, pitch-black skies teemed with dozens of glittering stars. Cool breezes brushed our faces as we headed down narrow walkways towards the dorm. Once inside the front door, we all said goodnight. It had been a long day for all of us.

Vanessa and I retreated to our room, a space not much bigger than a large walk-in closet, with barely enough room for our twin beds, two four-drawer dressers, and two modest-sized desks. The lack of space put privacy at a premium. Although I had experienced group living before, I never got used to undressing in front of someone else.

"If I get too nosy, say so and I'll back down," Vanessa said.

I quietly signaled my assent with a slight dip of my head.

"I hope we can be friends."

"I'm sure we can." I had a feeling she was genuine. The time was right for a good friend, but foster care had nearly eroded my ability to trust. Just when you get acclimated to one family, the agency thrust you into another unknown situation, often for a frivolous reason.

That night, I lay under the covers, staring at the darkened ceiling. I heard a few rumblings from next door, but within a short time, the entire dorm was quiet. Classes started the next day, and anxiety was in firm control. As a rule, I drifted off to dreamland not long after my head hit the pillow, but this night, I rolled about in bed for at least an hour before sleep finally came. I was ready to begin another chapter in my life.

CHAPTER 4

Life in a Big City

At dawn, the alarm clock roused me out of bed. Because I had volunteered to shower first, I had to be done by 6:15. Once dressed, I returned to wake Vanessa. An admitted late riser, she said it might take the boom of a marching band to wake her up. That was an understatement. I once pressed ice onto her ear lobes when my raised voice didn't do the trick. Breakfast in the cafeteria was served starting at 6:30, so once I saw Vanessa in an upright position, albeit with sleepy eyes and a flattened Afro, I assumed it was safe to leave.

Alone at a table fiddling with a cherry Pop Tart and a bowl of soggy corn flakes, I broke out into a cold sweat, worried about my first class. Thank God it was Introduction to Modern Literature and not math because I might have had a coronary or choked on my food.

I fretted about passing a literature class. Reading comprehension was like a nail constantly jabbing my side, as it had been since early childhood. As a foster child, I often hid in the public library to escape the chaos at home. I started to read different books, but understanding what I read was difficult. I refused to ask for extra attention at school. Some of the nuns resented having me in their class anyway. I could not bear the idea someone would make fun of me because I needed help with reading. Special assistance in those days was rarely available and unwillingly given. Those who required it were disparaged as "retards." People like me, in downtrodden situations, were expected to pull themselves up by their bootstraps, except I had no boots.

The mountain of anxiety that had reduced me to an emotional pile of rubble leveled off by the time I walked out of my last class. Of the five courses I registered in, three met the first day. The other two, sociology and American history, were scheduled for later in the week. As always, I viewed everyone else as brighter than me, but I believed somehow I could pull through. A tutoring service was available and I would make use of it should I run into any snags.

On the food line, I met Vanessa, so we sat together. This time she told me about her life growing up with a single parent. In her case, though, the single parent was her father. "My mom never seemed comfortable as a wife and mother. One day she burnt the fish. My dad wasn't mad, but she sobbed for hours over some stupid pile of blackened porgies. After that night, she started taking long walks," Vanessa said. "One day, she didn't come back."

"What happened?"

"Dad assumed the worst. He called the police, but they wouldn't do anything until she was missing for 48 hours. My dad started the search on his own. That poor man pounded the neighborhood streets for two solid days and tracked down every single lead. I didn't realize how much he loved her."

Listening to Vanessa made me realize I was not the only child who faced parental abandonment. For years, I had tried to blot out the mangled memories from my childhood that haunted me, especially in my dreams. Vanessa and I traveled together along the same lonely path. The big difference was I never got off the road.

"A bartender broke the bad news. Mom skipped town with a man from Los Angeles. We never saw or heard from her after that. I always thought I did something wrong."

"I felt like that a lot, too."

"Daddy told me it wasn't because of me, but children don't understand."

I considered opening up to her, but I was still too leery. What would happen if we became close? I immediately changed the subject. Vanessa seemed like she adored her father, so I assumed she'd be thrilled to talk about him.

I asked, "How was it being raised by your dad?"

"I wasn't exactly raised alone. Grandma Effie and Johnetta, one of my cousins who lived with her, moved in. Dad worked two jobs, so we had clean clothes and decent food. Grandma took us to school and picked us up every day. She kept a close eye on the both of us, and I mean close. If boys so much as looked at us, she either yelled or chased them with a broom."

"Are they still in Harlem?"

Emotion snagged Vanessa's voice. "Grandma passed last year. If it hadn't been for her, who knows what would've happened to us?" She wiped away the tears with a napkin and continued, "Johnnie went to Howard University and plans to become a doctor. My dad still lives in Harlem. He says that's the only home he's ever known and refuses to leave. Maybe you'll get to meet him someday."

"That'd be nice."

Since my first day went over smoothly, I had high hopes for the second. Showered, dressed and in the dining hall by 6:30 a.m., I studied while nibbling on a strip of fatty bacon and loosely scrambled eggs. Even the bland taste of powdered eggs did not bother me. If I read each paragraph twice and jotted down the key points, I was able to make sense of the important points. I trusted this technique to get me through the next four years.

These early moments of satisfaction ended abruptly in history class. Professor Clarice

Sedgewick, a wrinkled white woman with gray hair pulled back into a tight bun, had a glare that could melt the paint off a Chevy. I was the only black in a class of about 35 students. I sensed I was off to a rocky start when she offhandedly remarked, looking directly at me, that "you people" would have to work extra hard.

Should I defend myself, address her ignorance or lay low? I felt like a coward, but for someone so thin, Sedgewick was as intimidating as a nose tackle. I said nothing.

During her first lecture, she spoke with absolutely no emotion in her voice. "We will be studying American history from World War I to the present. Attendance is mandatory and so is this class if you want to graduate. No excuses for missing class. If you're sick, you must obtain a note from your doctor." Staring directly at me through her pince-nez glasses, her eyes were as sharp as ice picks. "For those who cannot afford a private doctor, a note from the school infirmary will do."

A young man with red hair and a distinctive Southern drawl asked, "Ma'am, what about grades?"

"I was about to get to that before you interrupted me." She wrapped her bony arms around her chest and glared at the young man like he was a child molester. "There will be two exams and a final paper, so learn how to use English properly. Attendance counts as part of your grade. Anyone absent more than twice is in for trouble."

Was a whipping in store for three unexcused absences?

"Your grade drops a letter." She stared at me again and said, "That is, you will start with a letter grade of B. If you miss three classes you have a C and so on. Class participation counts for 10% of your final grade. Does everyone get the picture?"

We all nodded our heads in the affirmative, but no one uttered a word.

"No talking in class unless you raise your hand. No gum chewing. I absolutely detest gum. And do not, I said do not, be late, not even by five seconds. Once I start to lecture, the door will be shut. Don't bother coming in when that happens. Any and all lateness will be considered an absence."

On the way out, the red-haired kid with the drawl called her an "iceberg." I chuckled silently and agreed with him 100 percent. But instead of starting a conversation with a guy I thought was cute, I hurried off. As a southerner, I figured, why would he want to talk to me anyway?

I returned to my dorm feeling wounded by the professor's rudeness, but reminded myself that her ignorance was her problem, not mine. As soon as I entered the foyer the sound of loud voices sidetracked my thoughts. My roommates were immersed in bid whist, a lively card game popular among black folks. I had played a few times when I lived in Buffalo. Mrs. Woodson rarely socialized, but many of her neighbors had bid whist parties that generated more clamor than religious revivals.

Vanessa set down her cards and said, "Want to join us? Charmaine is getting ready to quit, and we need another player."

"Sure, deal me in." I doubted she would take no for an answer.

"How were your classes today?" Vanessa asked as she shuffled the deck.

I told them about Professor Sedgewick and warned them, if at all possible, not to enroll in her class.

"Maybe we should ask her to play cards with us," Vanessa said.

We all cracked up and continued to play.

By the time the game ended, the dining hall had closed.

Vanessa said, "Let's go out to eat."

That was enough socializing for one day. I declined a dinner invitation. Alone in my room, I dragged out my history book and started reading. Of all my classes, I expected this one would be the most troublesome. No way would I show up unprepared. I pored over pages about World War I and its devastating aftermath in Europe. Around midnight, when my eyes were bleary and my body begged for sleep, I shoved the book aside and pulled the covers over my head.

A cancelled class led me to the student center one afternoon. I thumbed through the Yellow Pages under listings for children's services. Images of those battered and abandoned boys and girls at the nun's residence still haunted me. Forgetting their sorry faces was impossible. After several calls to different agencies, I decided to check out the Sojourner Truth House (STH). I was impressed when I talked to the director on the phone—he sounded as if he really cared about children.

Sojourner Truth House was in the South End, a section of Boston abutting Roxbury. The South End was racially and economically mixed, a situation that was a rarity in Boston in the early 1970s. Some blocks had shabby brick buildings and littered streets, but others were polished and lacked any sign of poverty. A flourishing minority population existed in the area. When Martin Luther King, Jr. studied for a doctorate at Boston University, he lived in a row house in the South End.

I got off the bus only a few blocks from STH. With the address scribbled on a piece of paper, I walked around until I found the right place. I was surprised to see it was a storefront squeezed in between a pizza parlor and a Chinese restaurant. What STH lacked in physical structure was made up by its respected presence in the community. It offered an array of social services to poor and low-income people who lived in the area.

The director, a tall, well-built young man with skin the color of honey, met me at the front door. He looked down to make eye contact with me and said, "Hi, I'm John Dawson. We spoke on the phone. Welcome to Sojourner Truth House."

I extended my hand. "Thanks for having me."

"Please, come into my office so we can talk."

I trailed behind him as we passed through a

busy room. A dark-skinned young man taught writing skills to a group of youngsters. In the opposite corner sat several older men who were learning how to read. Two leggy teens unpacked boxes and loaded canned goods onto shelves.

Along the way, John removed a pair of wire-framed glasses from his breast pocket, put them on, and said, "The public schools don't get as much around here, so our children have to be better prepared. Not everyone can read and write. We take care of them here."

"I'm very impressed."

"It's not easy, but we keep this place running. We have to," he said. "Our people need us."

We stopped at his office, which turned out to be a cubicle no larger than a broom closet. A chipped wooden table served as his desk and it was cluttered with files, letters, and reports. The crooked walls were decorated with posters of famous blacks like Sojourner Truth, Martin Luther King Jr., Malcolm X, and George Washington Carver. He motioned for me to take a seat on a rickety chair.

John gave me a brief history about himself and STH and said, "I'm here to teach people how to help themselves." He sat back and said, "Before we continue, tell me about you. Who is Theresa Cameron?"

I assumed this question would come up, so I rehearsed a compact statement, leaving out signs of emotional scars. When I finished, John said, "Now I understand why you're eager to work with our children. I'm glad you want to help out around here." He shook my hand in a fatherly way. "Come, we'll set up a schedule for you. I hope you can start right away."

In no time, we had arranged a weekly tutoring class in reading to fit around my school schedule. For a long time, I wanted to give back, but I felt too emotionally drained to be of any use to anyone. Visiting the children under Sister Petrina's care changed all that.

Late one afternoon, I ran into Janet, now a senior in the honors program. Arms loaded with books, she flashed a big grin even though she was obviously in a hurry. "I've been thinking about you. How is everything?"

I felt like unloading my problems with Sedgewick, but I decided not to, at least for the moment. If I could not handle this troubling situation on my own, I would ask for her help. "I'm hanging in. What about you?"

"I'm graduating this year," Janet said.

"Looking for a job or applying to grad school?"

"Grad school. I'm up to my eyeballs studying for the GREs. I'm sorry we haven't had much time to spend together," she said. "What're you doing this evening? Want to have dinner?"

"I'd love to."

*   *   *

One morning, I found a note underneath my door, summoning me to the financial aid office. A long line snaked from the counter back to the exit, so I took my place at the end. Almost an hour later, my turn arrived.

A middle-aged woman wearing an ill-fitting wig and a flowered polyester blouse said, "Your parents must sign your financial aid forms."

"I don't know who my parents are. I was raised in foster homes. It should say so on my application."

Her wig was tilted to the side. Should I tell her? If I said something, I figured she would be either embarrassed or angered, so I focused on the stack of papers in front of her.

The woman shook her head so hard the wig nearly flew off. I laughed inside at her silly looks. But then she got ugly. She spoke to me as if I were deaf and loudly repeated the same request. "Miss, we need their signatures on this form to give you student aid. Have it back to us soon or we'll cancel your scholarship."

The woman's bellowing tipped off my background to those around me. I did not appreciate their stares. "How can I make it clear to you? I was raised in foster homes."

Was this woman dense or what? She persisted by making the same demand. "Are your parents unavailable? Even if they're divorced, we need their signatures."

I was on the verge of hurling my books across the counter. The frustrated clerk relayed my request for a supervisor, who settled the dilemma. To get out of the financial-aid office, I had to pass by a group of students who now knew my personal business. I was aggravated as well as humiliated. I hoped she bought a different wig.

Ever so slowly, I acclimated myself to campus life. The bathroom routine ran without major hitches, except for the morning when Vanessa overslept. I left her sitting up, but once I was out of sight, she rested her head on the pillow for a short snooze and fell into a deep slumber. On top of missing her shower, she also missed her first class. I bought an alarm clock, one shrill enough to pierce eardrums. From that day on, she never lingered in bed again.

No sooner had I adjusted than a new issue dropped into my lap. It was time to pledge a sorority. Of course, I knew what sororities and fraternities were, but I had never thought about them. Anxious talk about which ones to join buzzed around the dorm. Students seemed more concerned with pledge week than with grades or what subject to major in.

Since I started school, I had kept my distance from groups. In my junior year of high school, I played on a volleyball team, but quit when the coach, a nun with a cathedral-sized attitude, forced practice every afternoon followed by a lengthy prayer session. Fed up, I left a few weeks into the season. Because I had such a strong serve, Sister the Insufferable flew into a tantrum. Evidently, there was an intense rivalry among the local Catholic high schools, and this nun was determined to win the diocesan championship. Maybe she bet her rosary beads on it, who knows? Without me, the team's chances at a trophy were greatly reduced. She hounded me every day for weeks until she was finally caught by the principal threatening me with a reduced grade unless I changed my mind. That experience, plus my general reluctance to socialize, led me to avoid groups of all kinds. Until BC, I had largely succeeded.

Everyone warned me that choosing the "wrong" sorority was tantamount to jumping off a cliff, but I did not care one way or another. To me, pledging sororities was more for show than it was about social intimacy and mutual support.

Few others shared my apathy. Debate about groups with funny-sounding Greek names was more intense than that generated by the *Roe v. Wade* decision handed down earlier that year. I considered studying more important, so I made myself scarce whenever the subject of pledges arose. I pretended interest until choices had to be made.

Sororities were organized according to race, although there were no written rules saying so. Everyone assumed blacks would join black sororities; whites would sign up with white sororities and so on. To keep peace among my roommates, I agreed to join Alphabets something or another. I expected to attend one or two meetings and then quietly fade away.

The big day arrived. I was shocked to see my roommates squabbling for extra bathroom time. Charmaine was in the shower, yet Vanessa banged on the door and yelled, "Get your butt in gear. There's a line out here."

Charmaine called out, "I was here first."

Unimpressed, Vanessa stepped up the pressure. "Move your black ass, I need to get ready. Don't do this to me, Charmaine."

"In a minute. I'm not done."

"Finish in your room then."

"No, I can't," Charmaine said, "and this is my bathroom time anyway. So there."

"Don't give me that."

The bickering went on until I intervened and brought them to a mutually agreeable solution. Vanessa got the bathroom, and Charmaine finished dressing in her room.

For pledge day, everyone wore fancy blouses and skirts that were cleaned and pressed. Afros were picked out to the size of a classroom globe. Everyone dabbed face powder on their cheeks and a touch of red to their lips. All this to join a social club?

When Vanessa saw me dressed casually, her eyes came close to zooming out of her head. "Is that what you're wearing?"

I glanced down at my clean but faded jeans and baby blue knit sweater. "Why, is there a problem?"

"I thought maybe you'd wear something a little different. Nicer maybe."

"I don't have much else."

Vanessa now looked like she felt sorry for me. "You want to borrow some of my clothes?"

"I'm at least four inches taller than you are! If I put on your slacks, they'd be up above my ankles. I'd look *really* funny then."

"I wish you had told me earlier."

I asked, "Is it really such a big deal?"

"Big deal? This could be the most important day of your college career!"

My mouth almost dropped open when I learned the truth about the life of a pledge. It involved doing the more senior "sisters'" dirty laundry, ironing their blouses, dusting their furniture, and cleaning out their toilet bowls. Not my idea of fun! It reminded me of the times when, as a group-home resident, we had to cook, clean, and cater to the nuns. I went along back then because I was a minor and had nowhere else to live. There was no one to complain to, either. Like the bishop would have sided with us?

As an adult, however, I strongly objected to sucking up to other students, some only a year older than I was. And this was allegedly the most critical day in my college career? I did not think so.

Inside the sorority house, an air of haughtiness nearly suffocated me. The president, a self-important young woman whose face was so tight it looked like her makeup was glued on, barked out orders as if we were inmates. Sister Smug, who was as light as whole-wheat flour, glared at us darker-skinned women like we were rabid dogs. With an insolent flip of the hand, she sashayed in front of us and said, "And you three, sit over there."

Such crude treatment was not what I expected nor was it something I would tolerate, not even from other blacks. I was ready to walk out when one of my roommates silently motioned for me to stay. Reluctantly, I agreed so their chances for hitching on with this egotistical crowd would not be affected by my displeasure. But I made up my mind. No matter what was said about sororities, I would refuse to join, especially this one.

When I thought the worst of the insults had been hurled at us, Sister Smug's voice became even more pompous as she stared at me and said, "Some of you darker sisters are lucky we'd even consider letting you join us."

That did it. I held my tongue, but there was no way I would join. I already felt like a social misfit. How could I feel even more banished? I refused to join, and the subject never again arose among my roommates, nor did they belittle me for backing out.

Nerve-wracking history classes with Professor Sedgewick always brought me to the edge. When the semester started, I came with a respect for history, a frequently slighted subject with many lessons to offer. Earlier in the summer, I even considered history as a major. Discovering Professor Sedgewick was next in line for department chair led me to abandon that idea quickly. Still, I had to make it through her class without letting her insults rip into shreds what little self-esteem I had.

Class participation counted a mere 10% towards the final grade, but I figured I should speak up. My involvement, however, was far from spontaneous. Listening to Sedgwick's arguments, I mindfully chose several opportune moments to express myself.

One afternoon, as the Holocaust was being discussed, she expressed amazement when I gave the correct response to one of her questions. She had mentioned the work of a noted Holocaust scholar, who I correctly identified as Elie Wiesel. In front of the entire class, she exclaimed, "I'm surprised you knew that." I was embarrassed as well as infuriated. If I had defended myself, I doubt she would have taken it kindly. I had to sit there and pretend I was not insulted or hurt.

In the middle of that class about World War II, the freckle-faced young man with the Southern drawl and red hair brought up a cogent point.

"Ma'am, why was our military segregated when we were over there trying to kick Hitler's behind?"

Momentarily taken aback, she paced across the floor until she said, "First of all, the U.S. was not in Europe to 'kick Adolf Hitler's rear end,' as you put it. We were there to save the world from the wretched grasp of the Nazis. Haven't you figured that out by my lectures and from your textbook?"

"But ma'am, you still didn't say why our Army was segregated. That didn't seem right to me."

Professor Pompous made sure she caught my eye. "The Army was segregated because black soldiers were not as prepared as whites. In order to win, we had to maintain our military superiority." A quick escape came when Sedgewick glanced at the wall clock. It was two minutes until 3 p.m. Lucky for her class ended at 3. "Time to stop. Start the chapter about the Cold War." Professor Sedgewick led a cold war of her own.

On the way out, the redhead and I got into an amiable discussion. Lance was from a very affluent family in Georgia. His father owned a multi-million-dollar life insurance company with offices throughout the South. As we walked along a tree-lined pathway, I asked, "You're far from home, aren't you?"

"I wanted to get away from my folks, so that's why I came to Boston." Passing by an empty bench, Lance asked, "Feel like sitting down for a spell?"

Until now, I had never had a conversation with someone white from the South. Indeed, this Southerner did not meet bigotry standards, but the wounds inflicted on blacks were still fresh, as well as painful. Since Lance was such an earnest young man, I let go of my hesitancy and flopped down on a seat next to him. His relaxed attitude eased me into a lighthearted conversation. Among the topics we dug into were the New York Knicks' recent victory over the Los Angeles Lakers to win the N.B.A. championship, the seemingly endless war in Southeast Asia, and the popularity of the rock group War and their hit, "The World is a Ghetto." As we ran our mouths on and on, I felt my emotional tightness unwind, but nervousness quickly jolted me out of my seat. I found myself liking this young man, but I was scared at the same time. I checked my watch and said, "Time to go."

"But . . ."

Without saying good-bye, I spun around and threw myself into a crowd of students. How could I face my feelings? I lived much of my life as an emotional dud. I easily related to dying, but living? That was another matter for which I was totally unprepared.

Spending time at the STH made me forget about imbeciles like Sedgewick. Because she was a respected scholar at BC, I backed off from taking my concerns to the department chairman, an older white man on the verge of retirement. Hearsay suggested he was planning to work with Boston school board member Louise Day Hicks, who ran a nasty campaign to thwart desegregating the Boston public schools. Whether the rumors were true or simply vicious gossip, I figured it would be pointless to complain about a long-term professor who the school admired and planned to promote.

The Head Start program at STH became a regular Friday morning routine for me. Blending in with children was easy compared to the dread I felt with adults. Social situations made my mouth dry as sand, but around the children I felt relaxed and at ease. None of them asked about my background. All they wanted was attention. Each week, I read to them, hoping they would develop a fondness for books. Not every child would grow up to be an athlete or a movie star, so a college degree was the most realistic exit from poverty.

When I finished reading a Daffy Duck tale to a youngster named Jake, he sat with a contented smile on his round face. The little boy had chubby cheeks and skin the color of Hershey Kisses, but there was loneliness embedded in his brown eyes. "I like this," he said. "Come and read everyday? I like when you read to me."

"I go to college so I can't come every day."

Jake nodded he understood, but I am not sure he did. I thought about telling him that as a black student he would be expected to perform at a higher level, but I thought he was too young to understand. He already had enough to deal with. "Maybe your mom can read to you?"

The sad sack's big eyes got teary. "Mama can't afford any books."

I pulled Jake closer and held him for a few seconds. When I had asked my foster mother, Mrs. Woodson, to read to me, she railed against reading silly stories written by white people. She claimed black people had to struggle to make a living. Reading, she said, was a privilege reserved for whites.

Earlier, John Dawson told me Jake's single mother had two other children and lived in a crummy four-room apartment. The oldest child had cerebral palsy. Jake's mother worked six days a week as a hospital aide, and every extra dime she earned went for food, clothing, and medical expenses. His father had died the previous year without life insurance. Little wonder the woman had no time for Jake.

Every Friday morning when I arrived at STH, I made sure to read a few extra pages to Jake. As I turned the last page, I knew he did not understand why story time was over. Jake always tugged on my arm and asked, "You can't stay and read some more? Please? I be good, I promise."

"Jake, you're not a bad boy."

"Then why you leaving?"

How could I fill him with the emotional nourishment he lacked at home? I had never figured out how to do it for myself. "Because I have to be in school. Honey, I'll be back next week with new story books."

I was afraid of becoming too emotionally caught up with him. Young Jake reminded me so much of myself it brought back the solitude I felt in foster care. Like Jake, I lived in homes where my basic needs were met, but no one made me feel special. I saw myself as a boarder, separate from the foster family. Either I could shower Jake with extra attention or I could protect myself. Spending time with this child would soften the chaos in his life, but I threw up a shield. To continue as a volunteer, I had to detach myself. I hated doing that.

A delightfully cool autumn slowly changed into a frigid winter. Heavy snow blanketed Boston like it did in Buffalo. The skies were often cardboard gray for days on end. The start of winter ended my strolls through Chestnut Hill.

One particularly bone-chilling morning, Vanessa took notice of what I had on. The puzzled look in her eyes made me feel bad because I knew what she was about to say. "It's like the Arctic out there. Is that all you're wearing?"

"Well . . . yes . . . it is."

"Why aren't you dressed for the cold?"

"Vanessa, this is all I have."

Usually sleepy so early in the morning, Vanessa quickly sprang into action. "I have an extra coat."

"I appreciate your offer, but really, I'm fine."

I had very little extra money. The meal plan kept me out of soup kitchens. The $40 I earned from part-time work in the campus library paid for laundry powder, deodorant, shampoo, carfare, skin cream, and toothpaste. From my experience as an independent adolescent, I was adept at saving for emergencies. Every payday, I stashed away at least half of my check. There was not enough for a new coat, even a used one.

"Cool it with that fine business. I won't take no for an answer." She grabbed a brown-and-tan waist-length wool coat from the closet and shoved it my arms. "Is that why you've been staying in your room lately and not coming out with us?"

I was so thankful for her kindness. I was also grateful I wouldn't freeze. Winters in Boston, although not as rough as in Buffalo, were cold and blustery. "I didn't think anyone would notice."

"I did notice. Why didn't you come to me?"

"I don't want to burden you with my problems."

Vanessa tenderly squeezed my hand. "Asking for warm clothes in this cold isn't a burden. You'd do it for me, wouldn't you?"

"Sure, I would."

"Then take the coat and wear it."

"What else can I say but thank you?"

Once I buttoned up and grabbed my books, I was ready to go, feeling blessed to be in a coat this time and not a skimpy jacket. Vanessa called out, "I got an extra ticket to the Earth, Wind, and Fire concert. Are you interested?"

"I can't pay you for it until next week."

"I don't want money for it. I'd rather have you join us."

"OK, I'd like that." The tight nest of isolation I wove around myself was beginning to soften.

History class became more bearable after Lance and I struck up a friendship. We left together when class ended. I found him a very kind, affable young man who kept my mind off the nasty barbs Sedgewick shot in my direction. I was also smitten by his red hair and freckled face. As much as I tried to squash my feelings, I was slowly drawn towards this young man with his gracious manners.

One frigid afternoon as we sat in the cafeteria sipping hot chocolate, he asked, "Would you like to see a movie or something tonight?"

I flashed a shy grin, but stared down at the table. I couldn't look into his gorgeous green eyes. "OK."

"Great, I'll meet you at your dorm around 7 p.m."

"No, wait. I'll meet you."

I hesitated to meet him at my dorm because he was white. The other black students accepted that I occasionally ate dinner with white students, but going out on a date might have been pushing it. There was no shame involved, but who needed flack for seeing him? On the other hand, I never gave them a chance to appreciate him.

For the next several months, I went out with Lance frequently. Because it was the dead of winter, we usually went to the movies or out to eat. Once, he treated me to a Boston Celtics game. As fond as I was of him, I still shoved an emotional wedge between us. He never mistreated me, but I was afraid of liking him too much. My blockade only held out for so long.

On the way back from a downtown movie, he asked, "You feel like coming up to my room? I got some hot chocolate with marshmallows. My mom taught me how to cook, so I promise the chocolate will be good."

I did not reply at first.

"You want to come or not?"

My intellectual side hesitated, but a longing in my heart convinced me to accept. "Yes, I'd like that."

The mug of hot cocoa warmed my body, but my soul caved in to his charm. Lights dimmed, he caressed my face with his tender hands. He parted his lips and pressed them against my open mouth.

For the next hour, we kissed and hugged. It felt so good to have a sweet-tempered man drape his arms around my body. The depth of the passion it stirred surprised me. Until now, I had shut myself off from physical relations with anyone. I wanted to have them but was always too afraid of facing another loss.

Shirt hanging out of his jeans and hair mussed, Lance whispered in my ear, "My roommate is gone for the weekend. Would you like to stay?"

"We shouldn't do this."

"But I thought you were enjoying me."

"It's just that . . ."

"Is it my color?"

"I'm not ready for a commitment."

The emotional moment fizzled, so we both straightened our clothes. I felt like a crumb, but I didn't know how else to handle the situation. To protect myself, I had to hurt him. "I'll see you in class on Monday."

"Wait, don't go."

"I better."

He asked, "You sure?"

"It's late, really."

"I'll walk you."

I could tell he was disappointed, but I ducked out anyway. The cold winter air reinforced the unhappiness always trailing me, but race was not the only reason I ended the relationship.

On the last day of history class, fierce winds blew so strongly it felt like winter would never end.

I was so glad to wear Vanessa's coat. Lance and I traded awkward glances whenever we passed each other. Now that the semester was almost over, I wondered if I would ever see him again.

Sedgewick handed out our final papers. The course grade was scribbled on the back. Double vision formed in my eyes when I saw I received an A. I could hardly believe what I saw. As students prepared to leave, Sedgewick asked me to stick around for a moment. I doubt she wanted to wish me well. Once we were alone, she gave me one of her typical acerbic snarls and said, "You know, I've never given such a high grade to a black person before. Are you sure all the work was yours?"

On the spot, my brain could not work fast enough to find the right words to defend my race and myself. "Yes it was. I'm sorry you doubt me."

"If you say so."

Was it worth my while to stoop to her level against a baseless accusation? I decided it was not, so I said, "Time for me to go." I could've said something offensive, but that was out of character for me, so I walked away. I sizzled with anger, but I refused to let her know she had upset me.

On my way to the dining hall that evening, I ran into Vanessa. We sat down together and over baked chicken and white rice talked about our final grades. Like me, she ended the semester with A's and B's. Then she asked, "What're you doing for Christmas?"

"Nothing special. What about you?"

"Going to Harlem to spend the holiday with my dad." Vanessa's eyes lit up as she asked, "Want to come?"

Another concern hit me. "I don't have any nice clothes to wear or money for presents."

"No problem."

Two days later, we departed South Station on a bus for New York City. Five hours later, we pulled into Port Authority bus terminal. If I thought the crowds in Boston were overpowering, the scene in New York City almost knocked me down. This was the most hectic, fast-paced city I had ever been in, and we hadn't even left the terminal. Vanessa caught my panic and held onto my arm as if I was a small child. "Don't get lost on me."

"Not to worry. I won't leave your side, not even for a minute. How did you survive growing up here?"

"You get used to it."

To reach Harlem, we rode the uptown A train, made famous by Duke Ellington's song, "Take the A Train." Fortunately, our early afternoon arrival enabled us to bypass rush hour. Otherwise, I might have gone crazy traveling with frantic passengers pushing and shoving their way on and off overcrowded trains. I was surprised the train only made one stop before arriving on West 125th Street. Perhaps the subway system was more efficient than I had heard.

I asked Vanessa, "Why no stops between 59th Street and Harlem?"

"The subway system was built to make sure black

people didn't get off the train before Harlem."

"You're kidding."

"No, but you're in Harlem now. And I'm home."

Outside, I felt like a little girl, gazing at my surroundings with wide-open eyes. Although I had lived in mostly black neighborhoods, I had never seen this many black people in one place. Everywhere I looked there were black faces. Even a few streets were named after famous black people. It felt good to be in a community where we ran the show. As we ambled down West 125th Street, the heart and soul of Harlem, Vanessa pointed out a few famous landmarks, such as the site of the old Hotel Theresa and the once vibrant but now decaying Apollo Theatre. She also filled me in on some of Harlem's renowned past, especially the famous blacks like Zora Neale Hurston and Langston Hughes, who lived and thrived during the Harlem Renaissance.

"I had no idea it had this kind of history. Or was this big. Or so many people lived here. Or . . ."

"Girl, step on it. It's cold, and I don't want to freeze my fanny off."

The sight of so much decay soon tempered my enthusiasm. There were blocks of abandoned apartment buildings looking like burned out shells in Berlin at the end of World War II. Streets were riddled with potholes, and sidewalks had deep gashes in the concrete. The vacant stares of addicts panhandling on street corners made me further depressed, so I blocked out these sights as we walked along side streets where garbage cans overflowed and rats the size of cats scurried around the refuse. Finally, we entered the lobby of a six-story apartment building that, although unimpressive in design, did not look bruised and battered.

As soon as the elevator door popped open on the 6th floor, Mr. Hampton, a slight man with thinning hair, stood with a grin so wide I could feel the love he had for his daughter. The two embraced for such a long time they were oblivious to neighbors as they passed by. I stood holding our bags.

Gray-haired Mr. Hampton stepped back and smiled. "You must be Theresa. Come in, I've heard a lot about you."

I should have hugged his small frame, but I only extended my hand. "Thanks for inviting me to your home."

"Any friend of my daughter is a friend to me."

I found myself inside a tiny box-shaped one-bedroom apartment where steam barely spilled out from the radiator. A three-foot artificial tree decorated with bright red satin balls rested on a worn table inside the living room. Mr. Hampton said, "Keep your sweaters on. The city has been a little stingy lately with the heat."

Sensing Vanessa and her dad needed time alone, I asked if I could take a nap. Mr. Hampton had already prepared his bedroom for us, so I removed my coat then crashed onto his bed. I must have been tired because when I opened my eyes the sun had gone down. I fixed my hair and splashed cold water on my face. When I returned to the small yet cozy living room, my nose wiggled from the delicious aroma emanating from the kitchen. Seated on a sofa, Mr. Hampton watched the evening news, where a motley group of protestors held signs demanding Nixon's impeachment. He smiled at me and beckoned for me to join him on the couch. "Vanessa is working magic with the pots. Dinner will be ready soon. I hope you're hungry."

With Walter Cronkite's voice in the background and gospel music drifting out of the neighboring apartment, I listened to Mr. Hampton boast about his only child. Pictures of Vanessa ranging from childhood to high school graduation graced the walls, the coffee table, and the foyer. Her bronzed baby shoes sat on top of the oversized black and white TV set. I was touched by his devotion but simultaneously envious I didn't have a parent like him. "I'm glad you could join us. My niece Johnnie and her boyfriend are here from Alabama for the holidays, too. We'll be spending Christmas with them. They're staying over on Convent Avenue in Sugar Hill with his people. We can walk while I show you the sights."

"At least we don't have to ride the subway," I said.

"Aren't you interested in seeing Rockefeller Center, the Empire State Building, and the windows of those fancy stores on Fifth Avenue?"

"Not if I have to go through all those crowds."

"This old man will protect you."

As our visit wound down, I longed for it to keep going. I felt unhappy about leaving. Over the last few days, I had eaten myself into a stupor, laughed so hard my stomach hurt, and listened to dozens of stories about Harlem during better times. I also felt wrapped in the love of Vanessa's family and a stubborn community clinging to its pride. Sure, I was pleased to escape the madness of New York City, but I was in no rush to get away from the affection in Vanessa's family. Nothing could replace what I missed as a child, but the visit provided me with enough to keep going. I hoped I would some-day have people like this in my life. Maybe I would not always be crushed by heartache.

Once I returned to campus and settled into classes, I watched as Vanessa flowed smoothly into the college routine. She studied hard, dated a few young men, and socialized with our classmates. Her social calendar was always full while mine was usually bare. Like Vanessa, I hit the books all the time, but beyond that, our lives took a significant divergence. I was a recluse. Only with prodding from Vanessa did I mingle with my fellow students. Other than my brief encounter with Lance, I shied away from dating. I was an oddball throughout my youth, and college did nothing to change that. I wondered if I would always be hampered by a childhood of foster care. Though I had no physical handicap, I felt more disabled than a quadraplegic.

CHAPTER 5

Another Twist

By the time spring break arrived, I expected mild, sunny days would undo my protracted winter blues. I should have been used to the cold, having grown up in Buffalo when months of frigid weather doused my spirits. Nothing could lift my fog. From the time I arrived at BC, there were ups and downs, but the one sure thing in my life was a constant thread of loneliness. The aching for a supportive family and friends continued to gnaw at my soul. Lately, I felt even more detached than usual.

So I retreated to Cambridge hoping for a break. Not even the sight of aging hippies preaching free love around Harvard Square cheered me up. I should have been happy because my grades were above average. Conditions at my dorm were mostly congenial. I was not living on skid row. The food on the meal plan was edible. So why was my life so gloomy? The long hikes along the Charles River served as therapy, allowing me time to think. I felt compelled to make another change. That was, after all, the only constant in my life—change.

One night in the dining hall, I noticed Vanessa eating alone. As I approached her table, I felt my knees become as shaky as the bowl of cherry Jell-O on my tray. "Mind if I join you?"

She looked at me with question marks in her eyes. "Must be something going on if you're asking to join me for dinner. Usually, it's the other way around." Vanessa slid the trigonometry textbook to the side. "What's up?"

Picking at my plate of chili, I pushed the red beans around with my fork so many times Vanessa finally said, "Stop it. You're making me nervous."

"I was thinking . . ." I stared at the mound of white rice next to the chili, but I couldn't force the words out of my mouth.

"Thinking about what? Dying your Afro green? You're acting weirder than usual."

"I was thinking about going back to Buffalo."

Vanessa looked as if I said I wanted to apply for a job as a shepherd. "Are you crazy?" She rattled the tips of her fingers against the table. "Lord, help me deal with this crazy sister in front of me."

"I watch you around other people, especially the sisters, so I could be more like you, but I don't fit in," I said. "You get along with everyone, and I don't. You're so smooth and I'm so gawky."

"More like me! Be yourself, not me," Vanessa

LEARNING TO LIVE   **89**
LEARNING TO LIVE **89**

said. "If you gave people a chance, they might like you and vice versa."

"Buffalo is the only place I've ever called home. It may be a crummy place, but for me, it's home."

"You know people in Boston now," Vanessa said. "Aren't we friends?"

So much confusion shrouded me I could not find a way out. "I think I'd do better back in a more familiar setting."

"Girl, you're on a full scholarship! Why are you leaving? That's crazy," Vanessa said. "You talked to anyone else?"

"No, just you."

Vanessa rested her thin, soft hand on top of mine. "Make sure it's the right thing before you go telling the admissions office. I think some of those old fogies would be glad to see another black face walk out of here. If you do leave, and I hope you won't, make sure you keep in touch."

I forced a grin. "You'll be the first person I'll call when I get back." Did she believe me?

What had I done? Had a lifetime of foster care clouded my judgment? Was I no longer a rational person? It was a wrenching decision to leave BC. Here I was, ready to return on my own accord to a place where I had felt tormented. Maybe I could have tried harder at BC? Perhaps I should have sought professional help. Regardless of all the *what ifs* I could come up with, I was as lost as ever. Returning to Buffalo felt like my chance at normality. Or was I too impetuous, behaving like a foster child where nothing is ever certain? Why was I adding further confusion and instability to my life?

The day before the withdrawal deadline, I rode the subway out to the beach. The vast, amazing sea had a calming influence on me, but I could not untangle my emotions. For hours, I listened to waves smash against long stretches of sand and turn into foam, disappearing anonymously into the ocean. That was how I felt. I had arrived at BC with a lot of energy and a strong desire to succeed. I rode on an emotional wave. Instead of forging ahead with my dreams, I slipped anonymously into a vast student body where I could not find my way around. Knowing I could not swim, I considered walking into the Atlantic that day as a way out of my dilemma. Drowning described my whole life anyway, but suicide was against Catholic Church doctrine.

In a grade school class many years earlier, the nun warned, "Only God has the right to take a life."

"If someone kills themselves, what happens? Does that make God mad?"

The nun jabbed her finger in my direction. I thought she wanted to poke me. Before she answered my question, she looked upward and blessed herself. "Those who commit suicide will suffer eternal pain."

"Will it hurt?"

"Why are you so interested in suicide anyway?"

"I was thinking."

The nun barged down the aisle, knocking over some kid's book. She glared at me as if I had said that the pope smoked grass. "God doesn't like it when people take their own lives. If you bring it up again, Missy, you'll go to the mother superior's office."

"Yes, sister."

"She's not happy when children talk back."

Keeping this in mind, I backed down. I had already found enough pain in this life, and I was only a little girl.

By the time I woke up the next morning, my mind was made up. I applied to the State University in Buffalo, and within two weeks, I was accepted as a transfer student. When I showed up at the admission's office to revoke my scholarship, I could hardly control my clammy hands. I dropped the pen at least four times, but I finally signed my name to the form.

The staff at STH threw me a going away party complete with a farewell card designed and signed by all the children. I was surprised by all the good-bye hugs I received. Momentarily, I regretted my decision. John Dawson pulled me to the side. "We're sorry you're leaving. You've done a lot of good work around here."

"I'm glad I was able to help." I was surprised when people, some I barely knew, seemed to care that I was moving on.

Jake, who had been sitting in a corner, tugged on my sleeve. He handed me a card drawn with crayons and made from colored paper.

The card read, "Dear Theresa, I like the stories you read me. Bye for now, Love, your friend Jake."

How could I not feel touched? Tears formed in my eyes, but I refused to show more emotion. As soon as the choked-up feelings passed, I bent down and hugged Jake.

"Thank you for the card."

He sucked on his thumb. "OK." A few tears slid down his cheeks. "Why you leaving?"

"I'll miss you." I held him again. "I know you don't understand."

He remained silent, and his little body was as hard as a rock. "Don't go, please."

Further explanations would sail right over his head, so I decided it was time to leave. I thanked everyone for the card and the small gift. If I stayed, I might have changed my mind. To this day, I wonder what happened to Jake.

On my last morning, Vanessa watched me throw my meager belongings into a new suitcase she had surprised me with. She handed me one of those understanding grins. "Look at me and tell me you'll write."

I turned to face her. "I'll write."

She hugged me as she said, "Don't hand me a line of bull like a two-faced snooty sister."

"As soon as I have an address, I'll write to you."

I failed to keep my part of the bargain, and I never saw her again. I know she cared, and I always regretted I blew her away. And was I making the right decision?

CHAPTER 6

Buffalo, Round Two

Jeanne knew about my plans to return. When I called to let her know my arrival date, she asked, "Do you have a place to stay?"

"I'm working on it."

"Do you plan to sleep on a park bench?"

"I'll stay in a cheap motel until I find a place."

"What about campus housing?" Jeanne asked.

"I applied late so I'm on a waiting list."

"Want to stay with me?"

"What about Ed?"

Jeanne, very active in the Catholic Church, responded with incredulity. "Theresa, please. We're not married yet."

"I didn't mean to offend you."

"I have a pull-out couch. You interested?"

I hedged a bit. True, I sorely needed a Buffalo

address. I sensed Jeanne wanted to help, but I was hesitant. Living in such close quarters posed another quandary. It might compel me into unwanted personal conversations. Talking about myself was harder than sitting through a statistics course. Reality, nonetheless, convinced me to say yes. "I'll pay rent."

"Contribute for food and the light bill," Jeanne said, "and save your money for an apartment."

Relieved by and grateful for her generous offer, my response was constrained as always. "Thanks."

Summer was hot and muggy. Even though Buffalo felt like a swamp, I sipped on hot coffee as I sat in a café circling ads for low-rent apartments. Then, I heard a familiar voice. Lena Wilson, a young black woman whose family I had lived with in high school, stood behind me. If it had not been for the Wilson family, I would have been on the streets. During the few months I lived there, I found myself drawn to Mrs. Wilson, a motherly figure who showered me with warmth and guidance. We enjoyed many long talks together. I was like a growing plant needing water. I soaked up Mrs. Wilson's attention and began to flourish, but I was also very careful not to overstep family boundaries. From some of the jibes Lena threw at me, it was easy to figure out she was jealous. We were at odds so often I finally moved out in a huff. I always regretted that decision.

I expected distance, but there was none. Lena smiled. I was surprised yet pleased. When she sat down, I said, "I thought you were going to New York City to take up acting."

"I changed my mind. What're you doing here?"

"You go first," I said.

"My parents lectured me over and over about the importance of a college education. This went on for weeks and weeks. I got tired of constant speeches," Lena said. "Then I talked to friends who had moved to New York City. All of them worked as waiters, housemaids, or taxi drivers. Damn, girl, who needs a life like that?"

"I went to Boston, but I felt out of touch," I said. "So I came back."

"Most people leave this God-forsaken place." Lena frowned. "I'm sorry I didn't leave with my parents when they moved to Delaware."

"I couldn't feel at home in Boston. Maybe I didn't give it enough time," I said. "Guess I can't fret over what might have been."

"Are you going to the university?" Lena asked.

That is what local people called SUNY Buffalo. As high school students, most kids aspired to attend. Few wanted to go elsewhere. Among the state universities in New York, SUNY Buffalo had a solid reputation for academic excellence. A degree from SUNY Buffalo was not as prestigious as a diploma from the Ivy League, but it carried a lot of weight.

"Yes, I am, and I'm looking for a place to live."

"Want to live with me again?" Lena said.

I appreciated the offer but hesitated. "Remember what happened last time?"

"You have every right to be pissed off at me. I acted like a jerk." She broke eye contact with me and stared idly at the counter. Her voice lowered. "I didn't mean it."

"What happened is over."

"When can you move in?"

"Is today all right?"

I felt like an inconvenience to Jeanne, even though she insisted I was not. Still, I felt awkward sleeping on her pullout couch in the living room. I knew Lena had more space, so I told Jeanne I was moving. I hoped I did not hurt her feelings.

My housing crisis temporarily solved, I shifted to a job search because my funds were quickly evaporating. The next morning, I found Lena in the kitchen and we shared mugs of coffee. Simone, our third roommate, remained upstairs in bed. A night owl, she either stayed up late reading or watching old movies. Lena said she rarely rolled out of bed before noon.

In a robe and slippers, Lena lazily buttered a piece of wheat toast. Once she took a bite, she asked me, "Can you hang with us today?"

"Wish I could. My money will run out soon. I need to find a job."

"Don't worry about rent," Lena said as she casually nibbled on the last piece of toast. "Daddy takes care of that. I have it easy, don't I?"

Not knowing how to respond, I avoided the question by grabbing my coffee mug and walking over to the sink. I took the last swig, placed it inside the sink, and said, "Wish me luck."

"If you get back early, join us for a picnic."

"Perhaps."

I did not join them for a picnic, but I found part-time work that day. I interviewed for a position with an undertaker, but I settled for a cashier's job instead. Grand Union, a chain of supermarkets serving the northeast, seemed less eerie than working around the dearly departed, as the undertaker so solemnly referred to his clients during our discussion. Considering I had a preoccupation with death, I was surprised that the idea of working around dead people unnerved me. Maybe deep down I really wanted to live. But how?

September rolled around and I began my sophomore year at SUNY Buffalo. The campus was altogether different from Boston College. First, there was size. BC had the leisurely feel of a small town, whereas SUNY Buffalo hopped along more like a mid-sized city. Student enrollment was three times larger. BC drew students from around the U.S. and from a few foreign countries. On the other hand, students at Buffalo were primarily from New York State. Subsidies from the state kept tuition payments modest.

An older, staid institution, BC had a certain polished elegance to it. Many of the brick buildings on the leafy campus were unique in design and had character. A newer campus, Buffalo had a more traditional feel. Buildings were mostly box-like, constructed without much thought to decoration. Grounds were maintained and buildings were clean, but SUNY Buffalo probably looked like any other state college. The adjoining community, although not a slum, was far from the affluence of Chestnut Hill. BC was in the midst of a well-to-do residential community, while a lot of bars doing a brisk business were crammed in around SUNY Buffalo. None of these differences really mattered anyway because I was there to get an education, and not to compare campus architecture or social trends.

On the first day of registration, I ran into a quandary in addition to a mass of anxious students. The no-smoking movement at the time was virtually non-existent, so I had to stand in line at the registrar's office surrounded by a cloud of rancid tobacco smoke, worse than the deadly fumes the now-defunct factories once spit out. When my turn on line finally came, the clerk looked over my form and asked, "What's your major?"

"I don't have one." My temples throbbed and I was desperate for fresh air.

"Can't enroll without one."

Speechless, all I could do was stare at the heavily made-up young woman as she rapped her long, flaming red fingernails against the counter. The clicking noise made me even more nervous, and the pain in my head sharpened.

Again, she said, "Miss, you gotta have a major. University rules."

"Can't I have a little time to think?"

"Nope, you gotta say something." In between smacking a wad of gum, she said, "Hurry up lady, you're holding up my line."

On the spot, I decided. I still was not sure I would make it through college or why I was even there, so I chose sociology for my major. Why, I do not know, but I did. How could I dwell on the future when I sweated through each day? Red Nails stamped my form with an official SUNY Buffalo insignia and handed it back to me. I was now a 'soc' major. The minute I walked out of the office, I searched for a water fountain and took two aspirin.

To graduate on time, I signed up for a hefty load of liberal arts classes. For Native American history class I had a black woman as the instructor. The only other black teacher I'd ever had was in grammar school. Far from being a role model and a source of inspiration, that long-ago teacher, Mrs. Gooding, was a demon that tortured me. A 30ish woman with skin the color of a light brown paper bag, Mrs. Gooding ridiculed me because of my chocolate color.

She once said, "You might do better if you weren't so dark." Another time she referred to me as "you people," as if she herself were not black. That was not the end, though. At every opportunity, she derided my braided hairstyle, my social awkwardness, and, above all, my learning problems.

One day when I had trouble understanding a concept, she called me "stupid" in front of the whole class, almost all of whom were white. A few bratty girls glared at me with turned up noses, making me feel even more humiliated. Although I grew up poor and in all-black neighborhoods, people respected one another, especially the children. Miss Gooding, however, belied the lessons about black power resonating in the 1960s and 1970s. I was ashamed she treated a black child with such disdain.

Professor Evelyn Calloway, a black professor who appeared to be in her early 40s, was so different. Patient and thoughtful, she treated every student with respect, even the ones who threw annoying questions at her.

A smart-aleck student asked, "What's so important about Indians anyway? I thought we defeated them."

Professor Calloway met his eyes without showing anger or annoyance. "Native American history is important to all of us."

That same student said, "Well, who cares, really?"

"Sir, this class is an elective. Students who are here want to learn about their history. If it's not what you want, I suggest you drop out and enroll in some other course."

She never lost her cool, even though I thought the guy was a narrow-minded oaf. I knew people who would have knocked his teeth out.

At least 45 students registered for the class, so individual attention was at a premium. It did not matter because in such a large class I was not about to raise my hand anyway. My shyness must have caught her attention because Professor Calloway made efforts to draw me out of myself. Always being prepared for class allowed me to contribute, yet I consistently offered curt replies.

One day after class she approached me with a tactful question. "You're one of my more quiet students in class. I wondered if you had any questions."

I returned the courtesy, but still, I was hardly forthcoming. "No, not really."

"I want to make sure you're following all my lectures. Some of the material gets complicated."

"Thank you for asking."

"If you need help with this class or any other, call on me," Professor Calloway said.

"OK."

Once in a while, we talked after class, but conversations were always cut short because she was a popular teacher. Other students demanded her time as well. She was probably exasperated with me anyway. I left her class not only with knowledge about a culture I knew little about, but also faith that not all black teachers were like Mrs. Gooding.

To avoid coming across as totally weird and anti-social, I befriended a student named Jill. Like me, Jill was a sophomore. She also had skin as dark as mahogany. We met during registration.

Over hot chocolate in the campus cafeteria, she filled me in on herself. "My Brooklyn neighborhood looks like one of those villages the U.S. flattened in Vietnam."

I, too, was raised in poverty, but it was more benign than in big cities. The neighborhoods where I lived had their share of crime and substandard housing, but they did not resemble hell. "I've only heard about places like that."

"My sister calls it a 24-hour pharmacy because so many drugs are sold there. Day and night. Night and day. The lines never seem to stop."

"For real?"

"The biggest employer is the drug trade. Most people don't have jobs because they dropped out of school and have few skills. Houses are no better than the shacks down South. Grocery stores carry outdated food and charge too much. And the sad thing is people seemed strangled by indifference," Jill said. "When I was a little girl, my parents swore they'd help me escape. They made sure I always went to school and did my homework."

"I had plenty of teachers who thought black kids were stupid. And when you mentioned college, their mouths dropped open," I said.

"Yeah girl, I hear that," Jill said. "I know *that* look very well. When I told my guidance counselor I was applying here, she almost laughed. She suggested I apply to a local community college, where she said the work was easier for students like me. I never thought I'd say this, but I may go back to the neighborhood some day."

"Why? I thought you hated it."

"After medical school, I plan to open a clinic, so poor people can get treated with dignity. The place we went to was overcrowded, understaffed, and run by people who didn't care whether we lived or died."

"I've been to lots of places like that."

"If we don't help ourselves then why should anybody else?" Jill said.

I agreed to hook up with Jill and her friends a few times each week for meals. As off-campus students, we gratefully avoided the meal plan. I heard the food was the same that was served in New York State prisons. To our misfortune, none of us were blessed with culinary talent. That left us with the option of eating in the fast food restaurants and greasy spoons wrapped around the campus.

Our first meal together turned out to be more than eating hamburgers and fries. As soon as we entered the corner diner, I headed towards an empty, clean table for four. Jill, however, nudged me to a messy table that obviously had not been bussed yet. I wondered why anyone would choose a table full of dirty plates over a clean one. I soon found out.

Making sure the coast was clear, Jill pocketed three singles the previous party had left as a tip and stuffed them inside her jeans. She took notice of my disapproving glance and said, "It's not what you think."

"What is it then?"

"I do this so I can pay my bill."

"What if you get caught?" I asked. "Won't it affect your school record?"

"Nobody ever sees me."

"Don't you think the waitress needs the

money?"

"Don't hand me a guilt trip."

Sure enough, she kept her word and used the tip money to settle her bill at the diner. Nonetheless, I felt uneasy that she stole someone's tips. Also, I was concerned about being dragged into theft charges. Dealing with the police was not what I had in mind. Besides that, I hated to see a black student giving weight to the stereotype that we were dishonest. My goal was to graduate and not end up in trouble because of Jill's illegal behavior. I easily related to Jill's financial woes, but I would not steal.

"Do you get financial aid?" I asked.

"Get real, I can barely get by with that little bit of money."

"What about a part-time job?"

"Don't get on my case."

I needed a diplomatic way out. I was too ashamed to eat with her, but I doubted she would understand if I told her the truth. Over the next few weeks, I cut back on the number of times we ate together. Instead of several times a week, my involvement dwindled to once or twice a month until I stopped going altogether. Jill never asked me why. I think she knew.

As a student pinched by a tight budget, I was always one step away from the poor house. Part of my tuition package included work-study. I ended up at the campus daycare center, which provided free baby-sitting for students, faculty, and staff members. I felt lucky to land this job because

Simone, one of my roommates, had the unlucky fortune to draw a position washing and folding towels for gym classes.

On my first day at the daycare center, I was taken by the free and easy attitude. The relaxed atmosphere was far from the inflexibility that ruled my childhood. I questioned whether a hippie philosophy was practical for children. Would the youngsters grow up wearing flowers in their hair, holding sit-ins, and flashing peace signs?

The supervisor, a tall, lanky man wearing a ponytail, met me at the door on my first day. When he introduced himself as Moon, I said, "Moon, what?"

"Moon is my name," he said in a voice so spacey I felt he was from another world. What the heck was this? Black people would never leave their child with a sitter named Moon who talked as if he was floating through the clouds. I did not know whether to laugh or call for help.

"What should I call you?"

"By my name," he said, looking down at the peace sign on his tie-dyed T-shirt. "Moon. M-O-O-N. I can tell from the look on your face you have doubts. Moon is a name that allows me to be in touch with my inner self. My wife is named Serenity, and we have an infant named Freedom."

Oh, God, why me? Had I ended up with more than my work requirement?

"The names are a little unusual, don't you think? Especially around here," I said. Buffalo was not Haight-Ashbury or Greenwich Village.

People were blue collar with a conservative way of thinking. They were not used to this. Names like Moon were a bit out of their league.

"Be free, my friend, and you'll see why some of us have these names."

I gave him a weird nod, but the more he talked the more I felt drawn to his way of thinking. He was unusual, but he was for real.

"I look forward to being here for my work-study."

Moon looked upwards, mumbled a few unintelligible words and held onto my hand. I was surprised by his gentle touch, considering he was over six feet tall. "No, it's not that simple. The children in our center won't be treated with many of the hang-ups you and I grew up with."

I certainly hoped that was true. The vagabond nature of multiple foster care placements loaded me down with more problems than I knew how to handle. "What do you mean?"

"Were you ever abused as a child?"

"I was hit a few times, but I wouldn't call it abuse."

"Children should not ever be hit by an adult," Moon said. "If anyone says they were punished like that, it's abuse. You were abused. Why were you hit?"

"When I soiled my pants."

Moon guided me through the center, passed the playful toddlers supervised by grinning adults wearing beads around their necks. "If you discourage a child from defecating, they grow up to be constipated. We want our children to be free with their feelings."

Did that mean free with their poop?

"We also do not yell. We sit down and talk about what is making us upset."

"I grew up around a lot of yelling."

Moon's eyes lit up. "And you didn't like it, right?"

"Yes, no, I mean no, I hated it."

"Precisely. Unkind words lead to all kinds of problems, ranging from poor self-esteem to war."

"Where did you learn this from?" I asked.

"From Martin Luther King, Jr. Mahatma Ghandi. Jesus Christ. They are my inspiration." Moon waited a second and then said, "We have a meditation group. Would you like to join us?"

I respected Moon and his way of thinking, but I wondered about fitting in with white people wearing tie-dyed T-shirts, beads, and faded bell-bottoms. "I have another job. Then there's studying. Thanks for asking."

"I see you're a nonbeliever." Moon rested his arm on my shoulder. "When you're ready to seek eternal peace, you'll join us. In the meantime, I'll see you next time. May the force of love follow you always."

At the end of our talk, I found myself in agreement with Moon's philosophy. The non-violent concept impressed me, even if I had trouble calling a grown man by the name of Moon.

*   *   *

My second job as a cashier was as dull as a presidential speech, but the weekly salary stretched the meager stipend I received from New York State. The grocery store, in a gritty working-class neighborhood, gave me a glimpse into lives shattered by continuing factory closures. Hardships over-shadowed the region, and I was motivated to acquire marketable skills to avoid the unemployment lines, which seemed to grow longer by the week.

A weary-looking white woman with shaggy brown hair came in late one afternoon with a trio of young, boisterous children. The haggard soul yelled, "Shut up, all of you."

One of the dirty-faced children whined. "Ma, I can't eat those junkie cookies you picked."

His older brother joined the chorus of vexation. "The dog won't even eat them."

Mom jabbed her finger in their faces. "You'll eat what we got. Not another word from you two."

Together, they said, "But ma . . ."

"But ma nothing."

When I rang up her groceries and said, "That'll be $24.98," she turned chalk white and fell silent. I sensed she did not have enough money. The youngest child wailed, the line of customers grew restless, and the woman looked like she needed a scotch and soda. Reaching into her shabby overcoat, she pulled out a wad of singles and, as I suspected, she came up four dollars short.

"Should I hold the groceries until you come back with more money?"

Tears welled in the woman's eyes. "I need all this stuff." The bottle hanging from the toddler's mouth was empty, and the woman's lips quivered. "My husband's unemployment ran out."

To keep the line moving, I thought of lending her money, but I only had two dollars in my pocket. I could not rush her, but the store manager's face got redder by the moment. He hated when the store got crowded, so I said, "Um, Miss, can you leave out a few things?"

"Like what, milk for the kids and meat for my husband? He likes meat at dinner."

"Have you considered food stamps?"

"We don't take handouts. Maybe you people do, but my husband has always worked."

Why was I being nice when she insulted me? I said, "Food stamps would be temporary—until your husband finds another job."

"The only offer he's had is from Woolworth's, but he can't support us on what little they pay."

I felt angry stares from customers waiting in line. "The manager is headed this way. He'll tell you to leave something or come back with the money."

The thick-necked manager barged in between the customer and me. "Listen up, lady. This is not a social service. I got a business to run. You're holding up my line."

"Because of you, goombah, we'll starve."

"Cooperate, will you?" the manager said.

The woman got the message and pointed to two cans of corned beef hash, a bag of bargain-brand cookies, and a large bottle of fruit punch.

She paid me in singles, all wet from perspiration. I wonder how she managed, living so close to the edge. Sometimes I wondered how I did, either.

Another roommate, Wendy, joined our household. From New York City, Wendy was also a sophomore, but she was white. Lena and Wendy sat next to one another in English Literature and shared a mutual distaste for *Beowulf*. Wendy got kicked out of her rundown apartment building when the bank foreclosed on the property, so Lena invited her to stay with us. Besides, we needed the money. Lena's father kicked in support as he had promised, but sometimes we fell behind on the utility bills. The cost of heating oil rose steadily, and so did our long-distance calls. Both Lena and our other roommate, Simone, had out-of-state boyfriends. A disconnect notice sent Lena to the downtown office where she hit them with a sob story. The ruse kept our phone line alive, but we could not avoid the late charges.

I came home from work and found Lena and Wendy sitting in the living room. Lena greeted me casually, as she always did. "Hey, Terry, glad you're here. Meet our new roommate."

I kept my coat on since the house was cold. To keep up with the heating bill, we kept the thermostat down, way down. I was my usual reserved self. I nodded politely at Wendy and said, "Good to meet you."

Wendy's bubbly personality made me nervous. No one can be that happy, especially living in Buffalo, New York in the dead of winter. As she jumped up to greet me, her wavy blonde hair bounced off her bony shoulders. "Hi, you must be Theresa. It's cool to meet you. Lena and I were talking. Want to join us?"

I had a thin smile. "No thanks."

Still in a Donna Reed mode, Wendy said, "I heated chicken pot pies for us, and there's one still on the stove. It wouldn't take me but a minute to fix it for you. You have to eat something."

"It's late."

"I don't mind cooking." Wendy broke away and headed for the kitchen.

"No, wait," I said.

"You don't like pot pies? I can make something else."

From the sofa, Lena studied the interaction taking place. I think she liked Wendy, but from the way she rolled her eyes around, she probably also saw our new roommate as a potential pest.

"I'll make toast," I said, "and that'll be fine."

"Are you sure?"

Lena grabbed Wendy by the hand and said, "Come on, girl, let's call it a night. You can cook for us on the weekend."

"I make a good lasagna," Wendy said.

"Goodnight, Wendy," I said, "see you in the morning."

Alone in the bare kitchen, I boiled water in a saucepan. Lena's mother had taken almost everything except for the old plastic picnic dishes, the on again/off again toaster, electric can opener, and assorted odds and ends. Gone also were the homey touches that once made the room the center of the household. There were no more houseplants, cookie jars, cookbooks, canisters or wicker baskets.

I sipped steaming Tetley tea, trapped in my thoughts. Eventually Wendy would find out I was raised in foster care, a subject that made me feel cold and empty. That was not in the textbooks, but it was what the system did after 19 years. Despite my efforts, I was sure a normal life would never be mine. Most people experience some chaos, but most everyone has a family. True, they may not like the cousin invited for Thanksgiving dinner or the aunt hosting the family reunion, but there was always the option to stay home. I had no such options. I did not know if I inherited any genetic disorders, or if I was related to a famous actress or a serial murderer. I felt disconnected from anyone and anything.

Winter finally loosened its grip. Snowstorms, where the snow was often measured in feet and not inches, slowly faded away. Temperatures inched up a notch every day. The campus became greener and less dreary. I put away my only winter coat and worn-out boots. Maybe by next year I would save enough for a new pair without leaks.

I felt increasingly restless. There was a place for me at someone's table, yet how could I find it? Students around me had plans to pursue careers in medicine, law, banking, anthropology, broadcasting and yes, even dental science. My profound fear of needles excluded medicine. Discomfort around people narrowed my possibilities. Computer programming might have been ideal, but I was lousy in math. I could not carry a note. I made good sandwiches but was otherwise inept in the kitchen. New opportunities continued to open up to minorities, but how did I fit in?

In hopes of getting a sense of direction, I made an appointment with Lucy Wiggins, a respected guidance counselor at the college. A smartly dressed professional, Wiggins wore a pale-yellow blouse, which, judging by the amount of spray starch had to be all cotton and custom laundered. Her black leather pumps had a bright sheen. She had on a gray, tailored skirt free of wrinkles. She gestured for me to sit down inside her likewise meticulously neat office.

"Good morning, Theresa," she said with a pleasant smile. "What can I do for you?"

A moment of silence passed. Then I said, "I don't know why I'm here."

"You said you wanted to talk about the rest of your college career. I've looked at your records and your grades seem fine. Do you want to drop out?"

"No, that's not it," I said. "I was thinking about a summer program."

"Why not study overseas?"

"Me? No, I can't do that."

"Why not?"

"Uhh . . . I don't know." I shrugged. "Because I guess I couldn't handle the work."

Wiggins picked up a manila folder from her desk and casually opened it. "Before you say no, read this through. Come back to see me in a week, and we'll talk some more."

"I don't speak a foreign language."

"There are overseas countries where English is spoken." She handed me the folder. "I'll see you next week."

Inside the hallway, I shoved the information inside my backpack and flew down the two flights of stairs. My next class was clear across campus, and I was already running late. During the sociology lecture about abnormal group behavior, my mind wandered. I browsed through the brochures outlining study in a foreign country. The programs intrigued me, and I seriously thought about applying. I was scared, but as Mrs. Wiggins said, what did I have to lose?

When my shift at the grocery store ended that gorgeous spring evening, I clocked out, grabbed my bag, and started walking. The cool night air was fresh and inviting. With so many smokestacks silenced forever, the midnight skies, splashed with dozens of gleaming stars, were incredibly clear. The protracted winter had halted my walks. Preoccupied, I was close to home before realizing I had covered several miles.

Once inside, I found Lena seated in the living room browsing through the latest issue of *Essence*. She said, "Hey girl."

I waved and asked, "Hey yourself. Where's Wendy?"

"With her boyfriend."

"Did she cook anything?"

"No. Why, you hungry?"

I let go of my bag and said, "Famished."

"You look tired, too. Busy night at the store?"

"Seemed as if the entire neighborhood did major food shopping tonight. I also walked home."

"Walked home!" Lena said. "From all the way over there?"

"I have a lot on my mind."

She motioned for me to join her on the sofa. "Feel like talking? And don't say 'no' like you always do."

I uttered a dry laugh. "You know me well."

"Tell me or I'll pry it out of you."

Out of my shoes, I unloaded my concerns about foreign study. "The program sounds good, but I don't know if I'll make it living in a foreign country."

"Have a better attitude," Lena said. "I feel a lot of negative energy around you. Keep an open mind and maybe it'll work out."

Lena's facial expression did an about-face from casual to solemn. She stared at me, like she was ready to spring bad news. "Why do you look like that?" I asked.

"I was wondering."

"Wondering what?" She floundered for so long, I became impatient and said, "What is it?"

"Don't you ever want to know about your family?"

Instead of backing away, like I always did when

anything too personal arose, I stayed with the conversation. I was, however, curt. "No."

"You're not curious about your mother? Your father? And people related to you?"

"Why? Should I be?"

"I'd want to know."

An edge came into my voice. "I don't consider the woman who gave birth to me as my mother. She's nothing. The man who provided the sperm is a donor, not my father."

"You never told me you felt like this."

"I keep it to myself."

"Why?"

"It brings up bad memories I'd rather keep hidden."

"You think of seeing somebody professional?" Lena asked.

"For what? I'm not crazy."

"I didn't say that, but you have a lot of shit to deal with."

"I know."

"Girl, I didn't mean to offend you," Lena said. "If I had your past, I'm not sure I could handle it."

"You do what you have to do."

I kept my distance from everyone, including her.

My body became cold and sweaty. Of course I wanted to know why I was abandoned as an infant, unable to defend myself against a welfare system stacked against black children. I spent my entire life blaming myself for something I had no control over.

Why would I want to meet the person responsible for throwing me into near lifelong depression?

I drew my feelings together so tightly that if you touched me I might have cracked. "Does it matter anymore?"

Lena must have sensed she was treading on very delicate ground. She backed off. "Feel like going for pizza?"

"Good idea."

She never raised the subject again.

I studied the booklet about college abroad. A year in a foreign country would be a challenge I felt ready to tackle. The application asked about preferences. Because of language, I considered the British Isles. There were schools in both England and Scotland, but I rejected them after learning more about the local weather. As it was, my life sagged under the blues. Living with steady rainfall would add to my depression. Then I thought about Scandinavia, where Ms. Wiggins assured me English was widely spoken. Denmark became my first preference.

A week later, I received a letter from Ms. Wiggins, saying, "Congratulations, you have been granted a one-year fellowship to study in Denmark at the University of Copenhagen."

Mrs. Wiggins told me about my host family. The Jurgensens, like all host families, had volunteered to house and feed me while I studied in Denmark. Married, in their mid-30s, the Jurgensens held civil-servant positions in the Danish government. They had two children, a nine-year-old boy, and a twelve-year-old girl. That's all Mrs. Wiggins knew about the Jurgensens. I trusted they knew I was black and that it would not be a problem. What would I do if it was?

Four students besides me were scheduled to spend a year in Denmark. On the day before we left, Ms. Wiggins met with us in her office.

"I may sound like your mother, but I say this to ALL students who leave for foreign exchange." Mrs. Wiggins folded her arms across her chest. "Be on your best behavior. You are representing SUNY Buffalo and the U.S. I don't expect to get reports about drunken or disorderly students. Obey all the Danish laws."

She stared at us for so long I knew she meant business. We looked at one another, and in unison we said, "Yes, Mrs. Wiggins."

"Good. I know you'll probably date, but watch yourselves. Look at me and say you understand what I mean." Mrs. Wiggins gave us a long, cool stare.

"Yes, Mrs. Wiggins," we said in unison, like a class of first graders.

"Don't be sloppy either. The Danes are an extremely neat and orderly people. Unlike us, they don't litter the streets with cigarette butts. Follow Danish culture. We don't want them to see us as slobs, which some of us unfortunately are."

Every so often she locked eyes with us. To

every admonition, we either nodded or said, "Yes, Mrs. Wiggins."

After a lengthy lecture about good behavior, birth control, alcohol abuse, personal hygiene, language, and food differences, Mrs. Wiggins smiled. "Good luck all of you. Call me if something comes up. Make the university proud of you."

That night, I shared dinner with Lena. We feasted on leftover chicken and dumplings Wendy had whipped up. Because Wendy was an excellent cook, we pooled our food money. Our live-in cook never tired of making us nutritious, tasty meals.

"Have a safe trip," Lena said.

"I'm sure it'll be fine." Underneath, I was a wreck, but my composed demeanor held up. "It's only for a year."

Lena stretched a grin. "I must be crazy, expecting you to show emotion. And I know you won't write or call."

"Maybe I'll break tradition," I said.

"I won't hold my breath. What about your stuff?" Lena asked.

"It's packed."

"Everything?"

"It all fit inside one suitcase," I said.

"What'll you do when you come back?"

"Finish school," I said.

"Want to come back here?"

I nodded that I did.

"I'll rent out your room, but unless I hear from you, I'll expect to see your black ass next year."

*   *   *

Early the next morning, I carried my only suit-case, caught a bus to the airport, and soon was on a plane to Copenhagen. I fretted about making the right choice. Would I fit in? What if I hated Denmark? Worry on top of worry gave me nausea. It was too late now to back out. I hoped the mounting wave of depression I kept running from would not crash down on me while I was in a foreign country.

CHAPTER 7

Denmark

On the short flight to New York's Kennedy Airport, we students sat apart. Transferring to a larger aircraft for the trip across the ocean, I met up with the other students, but my reserved self soon took over. Once we boarded the 747, I grabbed a seat next to a stranger. I hoped my classmates would not see me as distant, but I could not bear to spend so many hours making conversation with people I hardly knew. Maybe they would understand. They seemed excited while I was scared to death.

During the long trans-Atlantic flight, our stewardesses, all lean-bodied, blonde and blue-eyed young women, served typical Danish snacks. Our choices consisted of fresh and dried fruits, nuts, yogurt, and, of course, the popular Danish. These pastries were sweeter, flakier, and had more fruit than any Danish sold in the U.S. Served with hot coffee, they were scrumptious. Also available was an ample amount of alcohol. Beer, wine, cognac, and other spirits were handed out freely to any passenger who looked of age, perhaps as a way to keep us sedated since this was an overnight flight. I imagined the stewardesses were tired and wanted to catch a nap.

Even though I consumed several Danish pastries and a cup of hot coffee, I fell asleep and did not wake until I heard the pilot's voice. I hoped it was not news we were about to crash into the Atlantic. When the stewardesses reviewed safety procedures, I had neglected to pay attention.

In thickly accented English, the pilot announced, "Good morning, everyone. We are stopping for layover in Reykjavik, Iceland. We must refuel before continuing trip to Copenhagen."

I yawned and rubbed sleep from my eyes. Then the pilot said, "Please, everybody, we will only be half hour in Iceland. Do not go far."

At the Reykjavik airport, I met up with my colleagues. I felt uncomfortable around them, but I would have felt equally uncomfortable avoiding them. I joined them at a coffee shop. As they talked, I felt out of place when they rehashed their prior vacations in European hot spots such as the French Riviera and the Swiss Alps. These young people were the sons and daughters of affluent parents who worked as doctors, bankers, and lawyers. When the topic arose about my parents, I backed out of the conversation with, "Look at the time.

We don't want to miss our flight and get stuck here in Iceland." The ruse worked, and once again I avoided the topic of my unknown heritage.

Upon arrival in Copenhagen, I waited as one host family after another showed up to meet their host student. No one appeared for me.

A watchful airport employee said to me, "Miss, I am sorry to say, but the Jurgensens can not come and meet you."

She handed me a Danish State Railways schedule to their village and said, "This is for you. Please, you follow it." She nodded and walked away.

"Gee thanks," I thought sourly. Were the Jurgensens embarrassed because I was black? Not knowing anything about the status of race relations in Denmark, I tried to avoid placing too much emphasis on their absence. I convinced myself it was nothing. Perhaps their work schedule interfered with my arrival.

Another airport employee, slim, tall, blonde, and blue-eyed, must have seen the dazed look on my face as I tried to decipher the rail schedule. Acting very much like a gentleman, he asked, "Miss, do you need help?"

Danish names were usually long with many syllables. He chuckled when I tried to pronounce the name of the Jurgensens' village, so I showed him the schedule. "What time is the next train?" I asked.

"Because it's weekend, trains operate less often. The next one leaves in half hour." He treated me like any other traveler and directed me to the near-

by train station. At home, whites often shied away
when I approached them for directions. Sometimes,
they refused to respond, acting as if I was invis-
ible. Other times they recoiled in fear, as if I was a
thief.

"Thank you," I said.

"First time in Denmark?"

"Yes, it is. I'm here for college."

The worker, with hair so blonde it looked
white, frowned. "Your host family not meets you?"

I hung my head. "No, they did not."

"How rude for a Dane."

What should I have said?

"Good luck anyway, Miss. I hope you enjoy our
country."

"Thank you," I said as I walked away.

On my walk through the bustling terminal,
I was immediately impressed by a sense of order.
The few times I had been inside American airports, I recall being knocked over by tourists or
business people racing through crowded termi-
nals to catch flights. In Copenhagen the pace was
gradual yet steady. Danes showed respect for
elderly travelers and those with small children,
courtesies rare in the U.S. Smiling workers at
tiny, neat vending stands hawked dried fruit, nuts,
and yogurt. They did not have to compete with
greasy burgers or oily French fries sold in American
fast-food outlets. In the U.S., taxi stands and car-
rental agencies dominated airports, but I only saw
well-defined schedules for bus and train routes.
A small fleet of cabs, usually Saabs, Volvos or

Mercedes, was available but extremely expensive to ride in.

The airport was tastefully decorated in Scandinavian motif. Signs over stores were often colorful, made from hand-carved wood and lettered in Danish, French, German, and English. Window displays were full of handcrafted pottery with intricate details. I was awed by the refined nature of the airport. These decorations beat the factory-styled, cheap souvenirs and T-shirts sold in American airports.

The absence of cigarette use was most striking. As a non-smoker, I relished movement inside a large closed-in space without inhaling air made rancid from tobacco. I wondered when U.S. airports would catch on.

With few problems, I found my way to the airport train station. At the ticket booth, I took my place in a systematic line of weary passengers. My turn arrived and I asked, "When's the next train to Ingmar Village?"

"In fifteen minutes, Miss. You want a ticket?"

"Yes, please." At home, dark-skinned travelers were not always treated to such a luxury as courtesy. So far, so good, I thought. Denmark might not be such a bad place after all.

"*Goddag*," he said. Since he smiled as he handed me a ticket, I assumed he meant *good day*.

The aroma of fresh coffee from a nearby café enticed me to go in and take a seat. A young boy, drinking hot chocolate with his mother, seemed startled when he looked at me. I heard him say,

"Mama, what's the matter with her?"

The woman's red cheeks turned redder. She grabbed the little boy by the collar. "Sven, hush."

The mother tried to avoid eye contact with me, but her son, free from inhibitions, said again, "But mama, look at her. What's the . . ."

"Sven, stop it, I said. Be polite."

"She's got something wrong with her face."

"Sven, I said stop."

But Sven did not stop. His puzzled stares attracted more attention, making me feel like I was on display. Fortunately for me, the Danish train system is punctual. The piercing sound of a whistle as a train pulled into the station gave me an excuse to leave without ordering. Relieved to be off the spot, I nonetheless wondered if I would be regarded as a freak during my stay in Denmark. Was I really the first black person little Sven had ever seen?

The ride to Ingmar Village was so short I had no time to get nervous. When the conductor announced my stop, I took a deep breath, picked up my lone bag, and stepped off the train. My eyes wandered until I saw a family of four slowly approach me. I assumed they were my hosts. All wore casual dress—worn jeans, heavy wool cardigan sweaters, and clogs.

Their tense body movements suggested they were uncomfortable, so I said, "Hello, you must be the Jurgensens."

What forced smiles they offered seemed about as phony as America's promise for equality for the poor.

The father, a slim man with a thick head of blonde hair and blue eyes, said, "And you must be Theresa, *ja*. Welcome to Denmark. I'm Johan." Unlike the few other Danes I had met at the airport, he did not smile nor extend his hand, so neither did I.

"Thank you for having me," I said.

He traded fitful glances with his wife and children. "Please, meet my wife Gretchen. My son Karl and my daughter Liesel."

"It's a pleasure to meet you. I've heard a lot about you." That was a lie, of course. The school only told me I would be staying with a host family named Jurgensen. For all I knew, they could have been related to Hans Christian Anderson or small-time crooks.

The Jurgensens were cautiously polite. I was not sure if this was typical of Danish culture or a reflection of my skin color. Perhaps it was both. I tried to swallow my fears to get through this.

"Come, let us go," Johan said. "You must be tired."

I nodded that I was.

Gretchen offered to carry my bag, but I said, "No thanks, it's not very heavy."

I followed them in silence the way I followed a caseworker to a new foster home. Not knowing what to expect then or now, I focused on how I would get through this ordeal. I saw it as another step to my college degree, a piece of paper that would, I hope, keep me from a life mired in poverty.

As we left the train station, the mild temperatures surprised me. Denmark is at a northern latitude, so I expected the air to be cooler. I noticed only a few cars parked near the station, but a plethora of bus signs. We stood in line to wait for our bus. Except for Johan, who kept up the conversation, the family was somewhat aloof. I am sure I was, too.

During the ride, Johan said, "Will you join us for dinner?"

Exhausted from a long flight and anxious about my new surroundings, I was ready to crash. To please the Jurgensen family, however, I forced myself to say, "Of course, I'd be delighted to."

From the bus window, I saw quaint, colorful buildings on clean, cobblestone streets. Wooden and brick buildings displayed handcrafted carvings. There were no burned-out tenements, abandoned cars, boarded up storefronts or stray animals. People holding cloth shopping bags patronized what were family-owned stores. I saw none of the large chain stores that dominated the U.S., nor was I bombarded with ads for everything from suntan lotion to hot dogs. The most glaring difference between this suburb of Copenhagen and any American city was the lack of vehicular traffic. Americans would have been outraged. Bicyclists cruised along in a logical flow, showing respect for other riders. Most people nodded familiarity with one another. When people stopped and parked their bikes in front of a store, no one used locks. If they had done that in Buffalo, the bike would have been stolen by the time they walked down the first aisle. People smoked, but they stubbed their cigarettes inside ashtrays provided outside of shops and on street corners. I laughed, thinking how impossible that would be to implement in the U.S.

At the end of a brief trip, Johan nodded that our stop approached. The driver smiled politely as we exited the bus. "I hope you enjoy our country, Miss."

"I'm sure I will," I said, hoping I would.

As a foster child used to sudden and unexpected moves, I should have been acclimated to strange surroundings. This time, however, it was different because I was in a foreign country. Although most people spoke English, albeit heavily accented, they all looked alike to me. Almost everyone had blonde hair and blue eyes, and wore essentially the same type of casual clothes—blue jeans, clogs, and heavy knit sweaters. I felt more lost and alone than usual. Should I have stayed in the U.S.?

On our short walk from the bus stop to the Jurgensens' house, I paid attention to street names and other landmarks to avoid getting lost. I hoped strangers would be friendly if I had to ask directions.

Johan continued the forced conversation. "There is a bus that takes you to university." He pointed to the right. "Stops here."

"Thanks, I was about to ask that."

"Where are the other students staying?"

"I don't know. Their host families met them at

the airport and they left without saying good-bye. I'm sure I'll see them at the university." I did not intend to throw a dig at him for not meeting me at the airport, but I sensed Johan took it that way.

Staring straight ahead, he said, "Yes, that is so."

We arrived at their small brick house on a side street where everything looked similar. Front yards were neat but tiny, few houses had cars parked in the driveway, and most homes had window boxes overflowing with colorful flowers.

I was surprised when Johan opened the front door without a key. Doing so in the U.S. was an invitation to robbery, rape or even murder.

"Karl agreed to give you his room," Johan said. "He'll share Liesel's room."

I smiled at Karl. "Thank you."

He smiled back. "I am glad to do so."

I felt genuine concern from young Karl that I did not sense from his parents. That happened during my youth where children often welcomed me, but their parents showed fright at the idea of them playing with a black child.

The well-kept Jurgensen house was similar to upper-middle-class homes in the U.S., except it was considerably smaller. Even the kitchen appliances were compact. Wall-to-wall carpeting was replaced by wooden floors with scattered throw rugs. The living room had a working fireplace. There were a few pieces of Scandinavian-style furniture. Absent were the large, floor-model television sets the size of packing crates that so many Americans aspired to own. Already I liked the motif in Denmark much more than anything I had seen in Buffalo.

Once I freshened up, Gretchen said, "Please, Miss, it's time for dinner."

I did not like being called Miss, but other Danes had addressed me that way, so I did not take it as an insult. At least "Miss" showed more respect than the "n" word.

We sat around a small, circular wooden table and helped ourselves to a dish called *Hvid labskovs*, a Danish stew made from beef and boiled potatoes. Not liking the way the next dish, *kryddersild*, looked or smelled, I declined Johan's offer for a helping. Later I found out it was herring, a dish I never had a yen for.

As Johan passed the plate loaded with stew, he said, "We Danes eat a lot of beef and pork. Will this be a problem?"

"If you don't mind, I'll pass on the meat."

Gretchen smiled now and then, but she said little, except occasional admonishments to her children to be polite by not talking with their mouths full.

"You miss your family in America?" Karl asked.

I assumed the school did not inform the Jurgensens about my background. I swallowed a mouthful of potato and said, "I don't have one."

Poor Karl looked so incredulous. "Why not, Miss?"

Gretchen tried to quiet him. "Karl, don't be so

nosy. We just met her."

I offered him a cursory explanation of my past to which he replied, "I feel bad for you, Miss."

"That's OK. I'm used to it," I said. "Let's talk about something else."

Gretchen, meanwhile, served bowls of fresh fruit and yogurt for dessert before excusing herself to clean up. Unlike many modern American families, the Danes did not believe in dishwashers. Conservation was important to them long before there was talk of global warming, higher oil prices, and water shortages.

Karl, all smiles, said, "Want to know about my school?"

"Wait, let me tell her about mine," Liesel said.

Gretchen washed dishes in silence, and Johan retreated to the living room. While she rinsed, dried, and put away plates, silverware, and glasses, he turned on the record player. He listened to a symphony by Haydn.

For almost an hour, the two children rattled on about school, their friends, favorite subjects, and why they did not like sports, except for soccer. I felt a bond with them, one I did not feel with their parents.

Two days later, I rode the bus to the University of Copenhagen. There, I was directed to a lounge that resembled a conference room in a fancy hotel. This was the central meeting place for all foreign students, mostly white kids from the U.S. Crowds have always made me uncomfortable, so I searched the room for a friendly face. I exchanged casual greetings with the students from Buffalo and then noticed a handful of black students congregating in a corner. I gravitated towards them and met a tall, handsome man with a wispy mustache. He bent down and said, "My name is Jeff. Please join us."

A petite woman added, "I'm glad to see another sister among the crowd. My name is Lauren. All of us were just getting acquainted." She smiled at three other black women who stood nearby.

For the first time since I left Buffalo, I felt at ease. "Nice to meet you all. I'm Theresa. What school are you from?"

After we passed through the introductory rituals, we exchanged telephone numbers and addresses to stay in touch outside of the university. Announcements crackled over the loudspeaker to take our seats, so we promised to meet for lunch.

A blonde-haired man wearing khaki slacks, clogs, and a navy wool cardigan introduced himself as Hans, who had a last name so long I had no idea how to pronounce it. He was the director for the foreign-exchange program. "Good morning, all. Welcome to Denmark. We will break into small groups, learn about the program, and then start with class. *Ja?*" Hans whatever-his-name-was walked around the room and said, "Please, when your name is called go sit with that group."

The Danes evidently knew about the thorny history of integration in the U.S. because they evenly dispersed the black students among the groups, despite some whites who grimaced at the prospect of sitting so close to us. Perhaps the Danes were sensitive to American race relations because of what happened to Denmark during World War II. Germany invaded Denmark in 1940, but not until 1943 did the Nazis seize outright control. The Danes, who had declared neutrality at the beginning of war, vehemently resisted Nazi occupation. Unlike other European countries, Denmark rallied support around its Jewish citizens and the Danish resistance smuggled thousands to safely in nearby Sweden. I doubt the Danes would have accepted the often-violent nature of racial segregation as the natural order.

Senior Danish students supervised each of our groups. They handed out booklets containing useful information about Denmark, covering such topics as currency exchange, bank locations, postal regulations, places of interest, bus and train schedules, etc. Although most Danes spoke English, we were encouraged to learn a few common phrases such as *tak* for thank you, *ma jeg bede* for please (now that was a hard one to learn), and excuse me, which in Danish is *unkskyld*.

Classroom instruction was in Danish, so the university planned separate classes for us Americans. This form of segregation, I was told, was for my own good. Only time would tell if it was.

The fickle nature of foster care had pushed me into adapting to new routines during my youth. Settling into life in Denmark was harder because I was in a foreign country, surrounded by customs, people, and habits unfamiliar to me. The Jurgensens made my adjustment more difficult by treating me like a stranger rather than a welcome guest. Their stiff attitude did not help to ease my way into their home.

As a rule, we shared dinner three or four times a week. Other times I ate at the university or with Lauren and Jeff, the two black students I had befriended. Conversations with the Jurgensens were forced, but once in a while Johan brought up current events.

One evening, he said, "Have you run into any American dissidents since you are here? You know, men who didn't want to fight in Vietnam. A lot sought amnesty here. If they go home, they'll be arrested, *ja*?"

Richard Nixon was president so I replied, "I'm sure they would be. Can they stay here?"

"We Danes opposed the American aggression in Vietnam. We offered amnesty. Some men stayed, found work, married Danish women, and started families." Johan met my eyes with a cool stare. "Something not easy for foreigners."

Was Johan sending me a message? I had no plans to stay anyway. And if I decided to entertain such a move, I would not ask the Jurgensens to put me up.

Both Johan and Gretchen questioned the amount of time I spent in my room, asking why I did not go out more often. I did not feel like telling them I slept a lot because I was so depressed. Living in a foreign land without friends was not the only reason I had the blues. Many of my classmates had formed tight networks at the university. Others blended in with their Danish hosts. I could do neither. Years of isolation, along with a fractured substitute family life, left me a social invalid. My endless hours of sleep shielded me from my intense emotional pain.

About halfway through the semester, the Jurgensens stepped up their questions with a particular one that disturbed me.

Johan asked, "Why you don't go out with, you know, your own kind?"

Mind your own business, I thought. I had not experienced this type of ignorance since leaving the U.S. When blacks tried to integrate previously all-white neighborhoods, we were frequently met with idiotic statements like, "Stay with your own kind," or "You won't like it around here." When verbal intimidation failed, "For Sale" signs went up, and white neighbors fled to the suburbs. Those who stayed sometimes treated their new neighbors with jeers, burning crosses on their lawns, or sending rocks crashing through their windows. Blacks, like everyone else, wanted to live in decent housing, send their children to adequately staffed and well-equipped schools, and avoid crime. To do so often meant enduring daily onslaughts of racial epithets and sometimes violence from unhappy white residents. If we could have received those same services in the black community, most would have stayed. Who wanted to live amid fear and hostility all the time?

The first few weeks in Denmark provided a welcome respite from the almost daily racial intolerance I faced in the U.S. Hearing it from Johan and his wife soured my already shaky relationship with them.

I had to think for a few seconds before I responded. Finally, I said, "What do you mean, my own kind?"

Yes, I occasionally socialized with Lauren and Jeff, but that was none of their business.

Johan tried to extricate his foot from his mouth. "Other students, you know, the Americans. We are sorry you aren't happy here since you don't go out."

"I came here for an education, not to party. I hope you understand."

"*Ja, ja, ja.*" He said *ja* so many times he sounded like the Beatles singing the chorus to their song, "She Loves You."

I doubt he understood, nor did I care.

As winter set in and the temperatures dipped, I started closing the windows in my room. The Jurgensens were sparing with the heat. Shortly afterwards, I came home from school one afternoon and retreated to my room where I saw the curtains flapping in the wind. I was struck by the cold. The windows that I had closed in the morning were wide open. That was odd. I also did not like knowing my privacy had been invaded, so I confronted Gretchen in the kitchen.

"We Danes like fresh air," she said, dismissing

my concerns.

"But my room is freezing cold. It makes it hard for me to study," I said.

"Keep your sweater on. The air is good for you."

How could I argue with her? To keep the peace, I went along with her fresh air kick. The next day when I came in, my windows were again opened. All the other windows were closed. I wondered if she thought black people had body odor. I confronted her again.

"Hi, I heard what you said yesterday about fresh air," I said. "My windows are the only ones open. What's this all about?"

She looked stumped by my question. "Sorry, Miss, I forgot to close yours."

Several more times I found my windows open before Gretchen finally stopped. I never got an answer for her mysterious behavior. Maybe she really believed my presence tainted the room? Whatever her reason, those incidents left me feeling awkward.

After that night, I retreated to the library to complete my homework assignments instead of studying in my room. I felt disappointed by Johan's thoughtless comment and wondered why he and his family had decided to offer housing to a black student. Had they set up some kind of weird experiment?

I tried to avoid judging all Danes based on Johan and Gretchen. As a sociology major, I took courses on acceptable and unacceptable group behavior. I learned a lot about human conduct, merely from watching Danish society. Much of Danish culture impressed me. For example, Denmark had a wonderful social welfare network, extending from infancy to old age. Taxes were considerably higher than the U.S., but Danes had free access to day care, education, health care, and retirement homes. Imagine the uproar from insurance companies if the U.S. tried to implement socialized medicine.

The sense of safety surprised me as well. Crime happens everywhere, but for the most part Denmark was a much safer place to live than the U.S. When I was out after dark, I rarely worried. In some places in the U.S., only fools, criminals, or unlucky night workers stayed out after the sun set.

Recreational drug use was not regarded seriously in Danish society. Marijuana was not treated with the same draconian punishment as that handed out by American courts.

During one of our family dinners, Johan said, "We would never send someone to prison for life for marijuana. I can't believe they do so in your country."

"New York's Governor Rockefeller thinks that will deter people. It hasn't worked."

"Then why does he do it?"

"I don't know. Maybe to look like a tough guy."

"He looks like a fool," Johan said, grimacing.

Like most dinner conversations, the family deferred to Johan. The children were usually quiet around their parents, but otherwise they were quite talkative with me. Although I enjoyed the children's company, I thought about finding housing elsewhere.

In contrast to other European countries, Denmark had acted bravely during the war. It had rebuffed Hitler as much as possible for a small, essentially unarmed country. In keeping with that history, I thought Danes would display more equitable treatment to ethnic minorities. That, I found out, was not the case. At the university, for instance, racial tolerance was not what I expected. Some professors acted surprised when black students excelled. I had one professor who repeatedly called on white students even when I was the first to raise my hand.

A few white students obviously packed their racial prejudices and brought them along to Denmark. Hiding their tense feelings around blacks proved to be a struggle not all of them could manage. At lunch one day, I sat with a group of black women.

One acid-mouthed young man from Wisconsin threw a dig at us, loud enough for the entire cafeteria to hear. "They're only here because affirmative action paid for them. My father *paid* my way." He emphasized the word paid.

That snide comment rattled us, but we avoided a confrontation. If we let loose every time someone launched a verbal barb, we would be angry all the time. Thankfully, I did not share classes with him. Whenever I saw him in the cafeteria, I either sat in a far corner or ate outside. Eating in cold, wet weather was more inviting than getting daggers thrown at me from motor mouth.

There were dark-skinned people who lived in Denmark permanently. Most were guest workers from Spain and Greece, brought to fill jobs unwanted by most Danes. The darker-skinned people worked as busboys, taxi drivers, chambermaids, and housekeepers. There were no organized hate groups in Denmark like the KKK, but many Danes treated the guest workers as inferior. Because American blacks were mostly temporary residents, we were seen as less of a threat than the guest workers. Many Greeks and Spaniards married within their communities and bore children who attended Danish schools. Denmark needed unskilled labor, so the Danes had no choice but to live among the darker-skinned people. Not surprisingly, the guest workers were more likely to live in shabby housing in crowded neighborhoods. Conditions in no way mirrored slums in the U.S., but still, they were a blight upon the neat, orderly Danish society I had thus far seen.

At the end of classes on a chilly but sunny Friday afternoon, I ran into Jeff. Both of us needed a break from our grueling course loads. We decided to stash our books inside our lockers and go out.

As we waited for the downtown bus, he said, "Feel like going to the Tivoli?"

"What is it?"

"Girl, nobody has told you about the Tivoli?" Jeff chuckled. "It's a big tourist attraction in the heart of downtown Copenhagen. One of the sisters went there last week. She said the Tivoli has lots of restaurants, shops, flower gardens, and even amusement rides. Street performers, too."

"All of it sounds great except for the amusement rides." I then remembered my wallet, which was always close to empty. "Is it expensive?"

"Don't worry. I have money."

On our way into Copenhagen, I confided in Jeff about my situation with the Jurgensens. The host family he lived with sounded warm and welcoming, just the opposite. He said they lacked space for me, but added, "I'll help you look for another place."

"I feel so awkward there. Lately, the parents have started to speak Danish to each other and to the children in front of me," I said. "I'm not sure why they agreed to host me. I feel like I'm part of some weird social experiment."

The bus dropped us off only a few blocks from the Tivoli. This bustling entertainment center obviously had local as well as foreign appeal. Choosing a restaurant was hard because they all looked appealing. Jeff remembered the name of a place his classmate had mentioned. It offered good food at modest prices. The menu was in Danish with English translations. I ordered a green salad and French fries, while Jeff had the Danish version of the hamburger. Tempted by the sugary smell of Danish pastries, we both had a deliciously sweet *kringle*.

For several hours, we strolled about, gazing in store windows, watching children enjoy the rides, and laughing at some of the street performers.

We stayed until midnight, when the Tivoli closed. Despite the late hour, there were dozens of people lined up at the various bus stops, a sight rarely seen in the U.S. at such a late hour.

The bus reached my stop first. Jeff hugged me and said, "Try and hang in there."

"Thanks for a fun evening. Johan and Gretchen should be happy. I went out with my own kind."

Jeff and I both cracked up.

Towards the end of the semester, I probed my classmates about other sources of housing. After checking out several possibilities, I decided to move in with a married couple and their daughter. They had not signed up with the foreign student program, but they offered free room and board in exchange for tutoring their daughter in English and occasional childcare.

On my last night with the Jurgensens, I purposely stayed out till dark, hoping they would be finished with dinner. Several times that day I rehearsed how I would reveal my relocation plans. Then again, perhaps I worried needlessly. I didn't expect them to care. When I walked through the door, Johan and Gretchen were still in the kitchen, sipping hot chocolate. It had been cold and rainy all day. I interrupted their conversation and said, "I'd like to talk to you."

They both looked surprised.

"I'll be leaving in the morning."

"Where will you go? Isn't school still in session?" Johan asked. As usual, Gretchen deferred to her husband and let him do the talking.

"I think I'd be more comfortable somewhere else."

"We're not treating you well?" Johan seemed sorry about the news.

I had not expected his reaction. I hesitated then said, "I feel like I'm imposing on your family. Your son had to give up his room."

"That is what we agreed to." He looked at his wife. "But if that is what you want, then we accept your decision. We are sorry if you were not happy with us."

Lying in bed that night, I questioned my motives for moving. Was I truly uncomfortable with the Jurgensens, or was I simply unable to stay in one place very long? Would I always be rootless? I wondered if my adult life would be a string of address changes, just like my childhood. Would I ever be able to change that?

Early the next morning, I caught the family at the kitchen table, eating sweet rolls and orange slices. It was an awkward moment, but I thanked them for their hospitality. Holding onto my lone piece of luggage, I walked out the front door, hoping I had made the right choice.

*   *   *

The Hallen family, a middle-aged couple with a ten-year-old daughter, lived in a posh neighborhood in upscale Copenhagen. The expansive house, a combination of red brick and wood trim painted white, overlooked the shoreline. Salty water tickling my nose and the squawking of seagulls reminded me how much I loved the beach. Maybe this won't be so bad, I thought, as I walked along a short path of cobbled stones. I knocked on the door with a sweaty hand.

A slender woman with messy blonde hair pulled back into a bun appeared. She hurriedly yanked open the door, saying "Come in." Then she disappeared, leaving me stranded in the foyer. The wood floors looked as if they had recently been polished, so I removed my shoes. I had no idea what to do next. Glancing around for someone, anyone, I crept through the exquisitely furnished house until I found myself in the kitchen. There, a thin young girl sat at a wood table, eating yogurt out of a porcelain bowl.

"Excuse me," I said, "I'm your new tenant."

Without looking up, she said, "Hi, I'm Erika. Care for something to eat?" An open book of fairy tales, written by Hans Christian Andersen, rested to her right.

I wondered if she had known I was black.

"No thanks, but could I have a glass of water?"

Erika glanced at me then. "Want ice?" She seemed unmoved. Erika handed me a glass and said, "Mama said I'm supposed to show you to your room. Want to see it, Miss?"

I finally let go of my suitcase. "In a minute. Please, call me Theresa." I took a seat at the table. "Finish your yogurt and then take me to my room."

"Want to know about my school, Miss?"

I guess she could not help calling me Miss.

For the next half hour, Erika rattled on about a variety of issues, namely her favorite subjects, the Danish soccer team, her doting Aunt Inger and Uncle Lars in Sweden, her new bike, and the Odense Zoo (Denmark's second largest at the time). I wondered why her mother, Christina, wanted me to tutor Erika in English when the child's fluency was certainly much better than my limited command of Danish. My two most used words were *Jeg forstar*—I do not understand.

Erika boiled water for tea and brought out a plate of scrumptious Danish pastries. A flaky one with cherries called out my name, so I had to eat it. While we sat and talked, a blonde man wearing loose-fitting jeans, a bulky sweater, and clogs, even though it was cold, breezed through the kitchen. He grabbed a pastry and said, "Hi." He kissed Erika on the cheek and left, the pastry half in his mouth.

"That's Hans, my father. He's on his way to work," Erika said. "He's a doctor and works in hospital."

As late afternoon melted into evening, Erika and I ended up sharing dinner. She disliked eating meat as much as I did, so we feasted on fruit, fresh bread, nuts, and yogurt.

During dinner, I asked, "Where is your mom?"

Shrugging, she said, "I don't know. Maybe at the café. She goes there to talk about government.

She doesn't like conservative politicians. And she doesn't like Queen Margrethe."

Before leaving Buffalo, I did a little reading on Danish culture. Like England, the monarchy in Denmark was largely ceremonial. Still, the monarchy was a part of Danish culture.

"I thought the queen was popular," I said.

"Yes she is, but mama still doesn't like the royalty. Excuse me, Miss, for saying such a word, but mama says it's crap."

I chuckled as I thought about Richard Nixon ruling from a throne, surrounded by princes and princesses.

"Don't bring up politics around mama. She gets, how you say it, irr . . . i . . . tated."

"You have my word." I checked my wristwatch. "It's late. Can you show me to my room now?"

Life with the Hallen family was not much different from the Jurgensens. Unlike many Danish families who pride themselves on living in cozy homes that guests find comfortable, neither family shared that trait. Both homes were colder than the weather. The households felt like a collection of strangers, not family. I kept my distance from the Hallens, which was not hard to do.

*　　*　　*

Since I wanted to graduate early from Buffalo, I had to keep my studies on track. I had enrolled in additional courses to meet academic requirements at home. As lonely and isolated as I felt, I pushed myself to achieve in school. It was the only place I ever felt comfortable. In fact, while I was in Denmark I took the test for entry to American graduate school and passed. I applied to a university in the Midwest for their master's degree program, and I was accepted. Without a graduate degree, I feared I would have trouble securing a job to lift me out of poverty. A degree in sociology but no other marketable skills did not prepare me to compete in the workplace. Educated blacks were not immune to the bread line.

At the end of the semester, I had earned four A's and two B's. A group of us delayed our departure, so we could attend the Copenhagen Carnival, an annual event spread over three days and filled with traditional Danish dancing, music, and food. As festive as the occasion was, I went home with an aching feeling of sadness. I had earned good grades, but I still wondered if I would ever fit into life. Living for the past year in Denmark brought me no closer to that goal.

CHAPTER 8

Back in the U.S.A.

Before leaving Denmark, I wrote to my friend Lena, asking if she still had a spare room. A return letter welcomed me to live with her again, an offer I gladly accepted. Graduate classes at the university did not begin until late August, and I needed a roof over my head for the summer. Lucky for me Lena had space. I had nowhere else to go.

During my last few weeks in Denmark, I tutored a neighbor's seven-year-old son in English for extra money. I returned to the U.S. with $75 in my pocket, an amount I expected would be eaten up in no time.

After a grueling 12-hour journey that started with a train ride to Copenhagen, continued with a plane trip to New York City, and finally ended in

Buffalo, I arrived on Lena's doorstep, exhausted, hungry, and ready for bed. Lena, on the other hand, seemed ready to party.

"Hey girl. Look at your skinny self. Come in and tell me about Denmark," she said, dressed in bell-bottom jeans and platform shoes. The size of her Afro rivaled Angela Davis'.

"There's so much to tell," I said.

"So tell me," she said, smiling.

Since I knew Lena, I felt comfortable enough to shelve most of the conversation until tomorrow. I yawned and said, "Tomorrow I'll tell you everything."

"Oh, come on. I haven't seen you in almost a year and all you can say is 'I'm too tired.'" Lena made a face. "I have some cold cuts in the fridge. Fill me in while I make a roast beef sandwich. Want one?"

"Got any fruit?"

"You travel all the way from Europe and all you want is fruit? What'd they teach you over there?"

I told Lena about the impressive array of social welfare benefits all Danish citizens were entitled to. As I spoke about subsidized education from kindergarten to college, her eyes widened. Like me, she would graduate saddled with debt. "And when you get old enough for a nursing home, that's free too."

"Old folks' homes don't squeeze your life savings out of you?" she asked. "Then again, how many black people you know have life savings?"

"It's all provided. Education, day care, nursing

homes, health care," I said. "But it costs. They pay much higher taxes than we do; yet few people complain. Not like here."

She nodded. "As soon as a politician mentions tax hikes, he's booted out of office."

Sipping a soda, I said, "I'll tell you about their public transportation system tomorrow."

I stood up and dragged my tired self towards the door. I turned around when Lena said, "Girl, who cares about trains and buses. Meet any Danish men?"

"What do you think?"

"Knowing you, probably not."

The next morning, I showered, changed, and left before Lena awakened. On the bus ride downtown, the sight of decaying homes along rutted streets made me sad. As factories shut down and fled to countries with cheaper labor, the lifeblood of the surrounding community also vanished. Without customers, nearby businesses like restaurants, dry cleaners, and gas stations were also squeezed out. Buffalo, once a proud and mighty home of manufacturing, sputtered along like a car running out of gas.

I bought a newspaper and sat inside a tiny donut shop next to a group of unemployed middleaged men with grizzled faces. Together we sat silently, circling want ads. A knot tightened my stomach as I watched the men. Behind their blank expressions, I wondered if they were fretting over how to deal with mortgage payments and car loans when their unemployment benefits ran out.

I hoped to find an office job where I could use my college education, but I quickly found out a black woman with a degree in sociology from a state school was essentially no better off than a factory worker. I switched to Plan B and sought part-time employment. Jobs without benefits were more common.

After a lengthy day of interviews, I landed a part-time job at a dry cleaning shop in an affluent part of the city. Although it was a long bus ride from Lena's crumbling neighborhood, at least it guaranteed me a paycheck. Lena did not needle me for rent because her father still subsidized the mortgage payments. He put the house on the market, but only a handful of offers trickled in. None matched his asking price. At that time, most people moved out of Buffalo, not in. My stubborn pride, however, refused to accept Lena's charity, and I insisted on paying my own way.

Lena worked full-time, but on every weekend she club-hopped in popular discos, some nights dancing until dawn. Although she always invited me, I declined. On Saturday nights I laughed through the comedic scenes from *Saturday Night Live*. I particularly enjoyed the Not Ready for Prime Time Players: John Belushi, Bill Murray, Jane Curtin, Gilda Radner, Garrett Morris, and the others.

Only once, I yielded to Lena's persistent stabs at matchmaking and agreed to a blind date.

"It's better than staying in," Lena said.

"I don't mind staying in."

"Girl, trust me, I can set you up with a lot of fine looking brothers."

"Just this once," I said, certain I should have said no.

"Don't wear something hokey, OK? If you need an outfit, let me know. My closets are full of clothes."

When the young man strutted into our living room sporting a light blue sequined suit and white patent-leather shoes, boasting he was king of the disco, I gasped. At the end of our date, he puckered his lips and called me his Dixie peach. The next morning, I begged Lena to stay out of my love life.

Prior to leaving Denmark, Lauren, Jeff and I promised to stay in touch. Both had been supportive of me, even though I kept up my guard. Jeff returned to the West Coast, where he continued his education in California. Lauren went back to Massachusetts for her senior year. I am not a good correspondent, so I called them once or twice. I hoped I would keep up the friendships, as they both seemed like caring, thoughtful people. I suspected they had fallen in love in Denmark and wondered whether they would get married.

Throughout the summer, I attended school. Since I only enrolled in one course, my workload was light. I also worked part-time at the dry cleaners. After a week, I was moved from a presser to cashier. The owner liked me, but he said I took too much time ironing customers' clothes. Just as well. Working the pressing machine was so hot and steamy, I felt like I was in a jungle.

Jeanne and I had dinner now and then. On one occasion, she asked, "Do you need money?"

"I have a job," I said, not disclosing my occasional meals at the Salvation Army soup kitchen.

"I know, but you're going away to school soon. How are you going to survive?"

"I won a fellowship," I said, "that includes a stipend."

Jeanne's brow wrinkled. "Somehow, I don't think it'll be enough. If you need money, call me."

I did not want to seem like I was in perpetual need of a handout, but I appreciated her thoughtfulness. "OK."

"Keep in touch, please. I worry about you."

I was glad someone did.

In mid-August, I packed my suitcase and boarded a Greyhound bus for the Midwest. I hoped I had what it took for graduate school. What other choice did I have?

CHAPTER 9

Moving Up in the Midwest

As the half-filled bus edged away from the depot, the burly driver greeted us like family. "Ladies and gentlemen, welcome aboard. My name is Sam. There are restrooms in the rear. I just had them cleaned. Remember, this is a no smoking bus. Anything I can do to make your ride more comfortable, please let me know." A few people groaned, but I silently applauded. Typically, smoking was restricted to the rear on interstate buses. Perhaps the driver had allergies.

"And one more thing, folks. I like a clean bus. Please pick up after yourselves. Your mother isn't here. Thank you for your attention and enjoy the ride."

I gazed out the window, feeling as barren as the bleak urban landscape we passed on our way out of town. A sky choked with dreary rain clouds further dampened my mood. The big news of the week was that Barbara Walters had signed a contract with ABC worth a million dollars per year. Not expecting any similar offers, I hoped a graduate degree would enhance my chances for meaningful employment. Although affirmative action programs afforded blacks educational and job opportunities previously off limits, I still feared fading away on skid row. Many young adults scarred by years of foster care landed in prisons and mental institutions or eked out marginal lives on public assistance. Would the same eventually happen to me?

The smooth drive along interstate highways with few scenic distractions lulled me to sleep. I woke up with my face pressed against the ice-cold window as the bus pulled into a rest stop somewhere in Ohio.

Feeling bored, I made small talk with an older black woman as we stepped off the bus. "Feels good to stretch and breathe fresh air."

"You got *that* right," the gray-haired woman said emphatically, clutching a handbag. Her warmth brought a tiny grin to my face.

"I hope the bathrooms are clean," I said, "I hate dirty toilets." I had lived in one foster home where housecleaning was the lowest priority. The foster mother did not lift a finger to clean. Whenever I did, she always told me not to bother.

"Child, nothing can be as dirty as those old colored restrooms down South. Oh boy, was they *nasty*."

"I heard those years were terrible," I said. I felt fortunate to have escaped the crushing blows dealt by Jim Crow.

"Count your blessings you never had to use one of them bathrooms. Lord, could I tell you stories," the woman said, shaking her head. "Amen them days are over."

A chill shot up my spine, realizing I could have been thrust into foster care in a racially unforgiving state like Alabama or Mississippi.

"What's your name?" she asked, extending her wrinkled hand.

"Theresa," I said. "And yours?"

"I am Mrs. Etta May Clark," she replied with dignity.

"Where you headed, Mrs. Clark?" I asked, pleased to have such pleasant company.

"Home to Memphis. Making a stop in Cleveland to see my sister, and my husband is meeting me there. Just come from a few weeks in Rochester visiting my grandchildren. Want to see pictures of my babies? My son Earl and his wife had twins. Their first."

We ambled together through the bustling rest station packed with weary travelers. I was glad for Etta May's company. She reminded me of the grandmother I never had.

The bathroom facilities were barely tolerable. I questioned the quality of food sold in vending machines, so I settled for a diet soda and a pack of overly salty peanuts. Hunger biting at my stomach would have to wait a little longer.

Back on the bus, we sat together. I listened to Etta May reminisce about her forty-year marriage to James, a man she met picking snap peas in the fields of southern Georgia. Her extended family of brothers, sisters, in-laws, aunts, uncles, cousins, distant cousins, etc. gathered on all the big holidays. She spoke so lovingly of her six children and seventeen grandchildren my eyes became teary.

Quickly, I turned aside and said, "Excuse me, I need to use the restroom again."

I lied. No way could I let her see the moistness in my eyes. A child welfare system bounded by race and religion kept me from ever knowing a family like Etta May Clark had. I ducked into the closet-sized bathroom, but soon regained my composure because of the stench.

"Child, you feeling sick or something?" Etta May asked when I returned.

"Bus rides make me queasy. A little rest and I'll feel fine," I said.

"Here's a tissue. Wipe your face," she said. "Let me know if you need anything."

Closing my eyes, I leaned my head back and pretended to sleep. I was, however, wide-awake. Fond stories about Etta May's family made me feel emotionally bankrupt. I guess I would spend a lifetime wondering about familial relationships that may have been, but never were. Could I ever rip myself out of depression?

An hour later, the bus arrived in Cleveland. Etta May rested her hand on mine and said, "You take care now. Have a safe trip wherever you headed." She winked and stepped off the bus. Through the window I watched as an elderly black man waving a cane greeted her. When she smiled like a new bride and kissed him on the cheek, I presumed that was James.

Prior to leaving Buffalo, I mulled over my living possibilities. The university had offered me a dorm room. I thought about off-campus housing, but thumbed through a brochure about a local co-op, a housing arrangement I learned about in Denmark. I worried that communal living might compromise my privacy. On the other hand, the low rent and my chronic unbalanced budget lured me to accept this arrangement. At least they promised me a semi-private room.

I qualified for a partial scholarship, but it barely covered tuition. Feeling fairly certain that no rich uncle was going to come out of the woodwork and offer me a handout, I took out another student loan. What's a little more debt, I thought. Since the national debt was close to a trillion dollars, I figured I could manage.

Hundreds of miles later, the near-empty bus arrived at my destination. Unlike many Midwestern cities still reeling from the aftereffects of 1960s race riots, factory closures, and fiscal neglect, this college town bore no obvious signs of urban decay. As much as I empathized with the plight of rotting cities like my hometown of Buffalo, I was relieved to take up residence in a bucolic setting like this, even if it was only for a while.

Guessing that the crime rate was low, I dared to hitch a ride to campus with another lost-looking student.

"Are you a freshman like me?" the freckle-faced young woman asked as we stood near a corner with our thumbs out.

"No, I'm here for graduate school."

"I'm sorry," she said with an awkward giggle. "Please don't be mad."

"It's ok."

"This is my first time away from home. I hope I'll make it here."

So did I. "What's your name?" I asked, sensitive to her apprehension but unwilling to share my own.

A local storeowner on the way home from church drove us the short distance to the university. After we got out of the car, we exchanged names and addresses and promises to keep in touch. As soon as I folded the scrap of paper and shoved it inside my back pocket, I doubted I would ever call this young woman. I wondered if she planned to call me.

Entering the sprawling campus made my palms sweat. I thought of the title song from the sitcom, *The Jeffersons*. I was "moving on up," but to a very uncertain situation. Surrounded by strangers, I faced a new set of rules and expectations. Could I manage? Despite the passage of time, the fear associated with change never stopped choking me.

Graduate students were left on their own to

make sense of the sprawling campus. Unlike incoming freshmen, no orientation or welcome meetings were planned for us. I had to find my class schedule, learn my way around, deal with the bureaucracy, and show up for class.

With nothing to do, I meandered among stunning redbrick buildings that possessed the regal majesty of Middle Ages Gothic architecture. Cool autumn winds scattered crisp red, gold, and orange leaves across the perfectly manicured landscape. Groups of students, nearly all of them white, sauntered along wide walkways that snaked through the campus. Everyone but me, it seemed, was engrossed in conversation. I wondered how or if I would find my place. Would I spend the rest of my life as an oddball?

Next thing I knew I found myself standing on the rickety doorstep of the co-op, a three-story brick house that looked like an old mansion. I knocked on the thick wooden front door with a sweaty palm. While I waited, I stared at the ornate carvings on the door.

A young man with a mop of curly brown hair answered. "Are you Theresa Cameron from Buffalo?" Despite his casual dress, he acted like the consummate professional.

"Yes."

"Welcome to our co-op," he said as he held open the door. "My name is Kendall J. Blackstone. Please, join me in the kitchen so I can explain the rules."

I noticed Kendall had the delicate hands of a surgeon as he gestured for me to take a seat. "May I offer you juice to drink?"

"No thanks, but I'd like a glass of diet soda, please."

Kendall frowned as if I had asked for a dry martini with an olive. "We don't serve that chemical poison here. Only natural drinks are available." I settled for ice water.

For the next half-hour, Kendall explained the house rules. Smoking, alcohol, drugs, and loud music were banned. Pets were not allowed. A clean-up schedule for the eight residents was posted weekly in the kitchen. Failure to comply unless excused due to sickness was grounds for eviction. All residents were vegetarians. Rent payable in cash was due on the first of the month. No exceptions.

"So, is this an acceptable arrangement?" Kendall asked, as he rinsed out his glass.

"Sounds good to me."

"Oh, one more thing," he said, wiping his hands on a towel. "Every Thursday at 6 p.m. we have an open-house meeting. Everyone has to be here. And everyone has to participate."

Not what I expected, but somehow I would have to manage. At this late date, the dorms were full, and I had no money for private housing. As long as my housemates did not get too personal, I would slide by.

Alone because my roommate Jane was out for the evening, I glanced at yesterday's newspaper. A deepening recession as well as the loss of taxpayers, both corporate and individual, was strapping the state budget. The legislature responded by slashing contributions to higher education, among other programs. What would happen if I no longer qualified for student aid? Would that squash my dreams for a master's degree? Having no extra resources, I made an impulse decision to double up on classes and finish the degree in one year. What the heck? I had no social life, so I presumed I could handle the extra work.

The next morning, I rose early to avoid Jane. Last evening, she came home late, and I feigned sleep. Eventually we would meet, but until I felt more comfortable, which I hoped would be soon, I kept to myself. Classes started in a few days, and I wanted to discover the campus. After a quick bowl of cold cereal and a glass of orange juice, I threw on my clothes and headed for the nearby university.

Despite a nip biting the air, I spent several hours ambling through the campus, making note of important landmarks. Suddenly, an ordinary sight threw me into a tizzy. Bright-eyed freshmen and their watchful parents toted suitcases, boxes, stereos, etc. into the dorms. With my feet feeling like lead, I stopped and stared at mothers and fathers lovingly helping their children make the transition from adolescence to young adulthood. Even though I accepted my abandonment, I always ached to be surrounded by a warm, concerned family. The love and caring in front of me tugged at my heart.

A young black woman passing by took notice and asked, "Sister, are you ok?"

A lemon-sized lump clogged my throat. I could not speak.

The stranger gently touched my arm and said, "Want me to help you to medical?"

Finally, I grabbed control of myself. "Uh, no thanks. I'm fine, really."

"You don't look fine. Are you sure?"

"Yes," I said, ignoring the ripples in my stomach. "I must have a bug or something."

"I'm Deidre. Maybe I'll see you again."

"Yeah, sure."

I watched Deidre melt into the crowd of students clogging the walkways. I headed for the nearest building to use the bathroom. I felt sick to my stomach. I never saw her again, either.

Among the urban planning classes I enrolled in were courses about housing analysis, land-use law, and community development, core courses for my housing concentration. When I'm asked to explain my field, urban planning, I compare it to a giant Day-Timer. As people who use Day-Timers know, these organizational tools list every aspect of one's day—meetings, luncheons, dental appointments, and so on. Without the Day-Timer, many of us would be lost, especially me. I would not know how to function without reminders of where I should be and at what time. If you carry this sense of order onto a much larger scale and relate it to various aspects of city life, that is urban planning.

Unfortunately, some American cities failed to follow sensible urban planning, and city sprawl resulted. Nowadays planners are trying to undo years of haphazard development that often harmed the environment and turned cities into miles of faceless strip malls, but that is another topic.

In line one day in the cafeteria, I ran into another black student. Henry introduced himself and said, "You look tired. Just come from a boring class?"

After telling him my name, I said, "Actually, no. I was in a community development class. I stayed up late last night to finish my project."

"Community development? What's that?"

Briefly, I explained the concept and its significance to city life. He raised his eyebrows incredulously as I talked. "You look skeptical," I remarked.

"How come nobody develops housing and business in poor black neighborhoods?" he asked. "Man, places like Watts, Harlem, and Detroit all need help."

He was right, they did.

"Politicians blab about urban renewal all the time, but nothing ever happens in our neighborhoods," Henry said. "Wonder if things will improve if Jimmy Carter is elected."

"They can't get much worse," I said.

"Yes they can."

I hoped he was not right.

Just after sunrise, I slipped out of bed and into my clothes. Again, I hoped to avoid Jane.

Not a morning person, Jane had registered for later classes. Holding my books in one arm, I snatched my jacket and tiptoed towards the door. But as I reached for the doorknob, a hand grabbed my arm.

"I caught you this time," she said. Yawning, Jane threw off the covers and jumped out of bed. "Stop sneaking out so early. I want to see you. We do share the same room."

I was embarrassed. "I have early classes."

"The earliest class begins at 8 o'clock. It's only after 6. Sit down and talk to me."

I hedged. "Now isn't a good time."

"The crack of dawn isn't good?"

"OK, I'll sit down, but only for a few minutes."

For the next half-hour, we talked. Like me, Jane was a graduate student. She majored in music. She came from an affluent suburb of Pittsburgh, and her parents paid for everything. Growing up, though, Jane's values differed from her family, and she had pursued a career as a jazz musician, often hooking up with black artists. Then came the dreaded question.

"What about your family?"

"I don't have one."

At least she did not shower me with condolences. Instead, she asked a few salient questions, all of which I answered. I decided to like her. If I relaxed my guard, we might even be friends.

Checking my watch, I said, "This time I really have to go. See you later."

"I'm going to a jazz club tonight. Want to come?"

"OK." I was surprised I agreed.

As I juggled course work and a part-time job, I maintained above-average grades. The near absence of a personal life and virtually no spending money kept me focused. Moreover, I enjoyed the urban planning curriculum. Perhaps it provided me with the sense of order missing from my youth.

On the whole, the professors in my department were competent as well as cordial. A few even extended themselves to help me complete a two-year program in one year. I appreciated the special attention and relished the guidance.

Only Professor Berk, a middle-aged man with a boulder-sized chip on his shoulder, viewed the handful of black students in the department as shiftless and inept. The mere mention of affirmative action made him squirm. Enrollment in his neighborhood planning class was required. Lucky me.

Supposedly, students in his class were randomly assigned to work in small groups. Interestingly, all three black students ended up together. Random?

For a class assignment we had to formulate a neighborhood plan by incorporating theories Professor Berk had taught us. Our urban plans had to include a concise policy statement as well as a way to evaluate results. For instance, an economic development plan would invest government and/or private funds to bring jobs, small businesses, and housing to a distressed area. The evaluation component would study the area to determine if the infusion of capital had actually helped revitalize the targeted area.

Our group chose to focus on a small rural town abandoned by its largest employer after a corporate takeover. In some ways, each group member had been affected by the steady disappearance of factories that had provided work. An automobile factory closure had caused one student's family to plunge into poverty when her parents lost their jobs. Another student lived in a southern town dominated for years by a sprawling cotton mill. When it ceased operations, her parents were thrown out of work and into the poorhouse. I had watched Buffalo slide from a solidly blue-collar town into a city rutted by decaying factories, empty storefronts, and scores of idle workers.

Predictably, Professor Berk's objections started as soon as we presented our plan.

"Why didn't you choose an inner city neighborhood, someplace in Detroit or Cleveland?" He scowled at the only three black faces in class.

Caught by surprise, none of us knew how to respond. We sat and listened as Berk ripped our plan into shreds. The semester had just begun.

"What's the amount of funding proposed?" he barked.

I took the lead and said, "Dr. Berk, I wasn't aware we had to tie down an amount so soon."

"What's the funding source? Government? Private? I'm waiting for an answer." He tapped his foot against the floor so quickly it sounded like a metronome.

A cold silence chilled the class. No one said a word. I wanted to scream.

An impatient snort from Professor Berk put me on the spot. Whether the other students liked us or not, they had to realize that the professor had grilled us for no reason. They could be next.

"Get that to me next time," he said, turning away from us. "Understand?" He talked as if we were imbeciles.

At least for a while, the negative attention was diverted. How soon would it return? Knowing I couldn't drop this class made my temples throb.

At the suggestion of a professor in my department, I sent a resume to a state representative. A few days later, he accepted my application for part-time employment.

A slender black man in his early 50s, Assemblyman John Lowe represented a largely black low-income constituency. Although Mr. Lowe never said so, I wondered if he had hired me because of my past. Over the years, I learned, he and his wife Linda had cared for at least ten foster children and had adopted four.

During an early discussion we had, he said, "All those children still keep in touch with us. Get Christmas cards from them every year."

I tried to smile. "That's nice."

"Do you ever keep in touch with your foster families?"

"No sir." Why would I when I felt so disconnected from them?

I was glad when he changed the subject. "I'm happy to say all my children are doing well. Most went to college. One went in the service. Not a single one got on drugs."

"That's good news, sir."

He seemed proud of his commitment to less-fortunate black children. People like Assemblyman Lowe added stability to foster care. I wish I had lived with a family like his.

In addition to me, his office employed a full-time secretary and at least two other part-time clerks, always college students. Volunteers worked in his office as well. As a newly hired clerk, I answered the telephone, sorted mail, and filed reports. The office was hectic and the work tedious, but I did not mind. Assemblyman Lowe treated everyone with respect and insisted his staff do likewise.

As the semester progressed, Jane and I shared a guarded friendship. I could loosen up but only so much. Now and then, we shared coffee at a cozy breakfast den in the downtown area. Both news junkies, we discussed the latest current events about the nuclear arms race, what Jimmy Carter would bring to the presidency, and the growing popularity of the Rev. Sun Yung Moon's Unification Church. From time to time, I broke with tradition and accompanied Jane to jazz clubs and listened to her play the piano. When I overcame my reserved nature, I enjoyed myself.

*   *   *

One morning as Jane and I drank coffee, she asked, "Do you have photos of your childhood?"

I shook my head. "No." That always made me sad.

"None? None at all? You seem so unconcerned." Jane's scrunched up face showed disbelief.

"I didn't have a childhood like most kids do. I moved from home to home so I didn't get attached to anything. Or anyone."

"Is that why your side of the room is so empty?"

I took a swig of coffee. "Yeah, I guess." I doubted that she understood. Sometimes, I did not either.

As they had promised, Jeff and Lauren, the two American students I befriended in Denmark, stayed in my life. I kept my part by calling, but not nearly as often as they sent cards and letters. I was surprised I did not turn them away, as I had with other people in my life. But I was not surprised to learn they had finally started living together. I thought it was only a matter of time before they got married.

The pressures of graduate school and a part-time job shoved me to the limit. I survived on about six hours of sleep a night. Every meal was consumed in haste. Perhaps I should not have been so paranoid about financial aid. Besides the daily grind, the constant barbs thrown by Dr. Berk frustrated me. Minor blunders that deserved only a mild admonition produced threats of failure. In front of faculty members, however, two-faced Professor Berk acted the role of a thoughtful professor.

"Theresa, don't forget to sign up for my office hours."

I would rather eat paste than be alone with him.

To me he was the notoriously bigoted Birmingham police chief Bull Connor in a three-piece suit. Instead of hosing down blacks with cascades of gushing water, this Bull Connor hosed us down with his pernicious attitude.

On the outside, my harried life seemed typical of a graduate student. Every day was consumed by classes, work, and studying. Surprisingly, I relaxed enough around Jane to enjoy her as a roommate. Eventually, I even reluctantly accepted an invitation to a party. Jane badgered me so much I couldn't say no. On our way to the party, I said, "I'm staying for an hour."

"Why not two?" she asked.

"I can't believe I'm going," I said, sulking as usual.

"Deep down you want the company, just like I do. You're not the sourpuss you make yourself out to be."

Maybe so, I thought. I just did not know any other way to act.

Entering a private house jam-packed with about fifty people, I started to perspire. Jane said there would only be a handful of students. "What are all these people doing here?" I asked.

"I guess the host invited more people than he said." Jane guided me through the narrow doorway. "Try it for a little while. If you're still uncomfortable, I won't be mad if you go home."

Squeezing through a swarm of people, I found an empty seat. I grabbed it, wondering how long I would last. Thirsty, I eyed the room, searching for cold sodas. As I was about to stand, a scholarly-looking young white man with a trimmed beard handed me a Coke. "You look like you need this."

I appreciated the kind gesture. "Thank you." Although I hadn't noticed him, he had obviously noticed me.

Playing it cool, he slid into the recently vacated chair next to me. "What's your name?"

"Theresa."

"I'm Steve," he said, extending his manicured hand. "Are you a student?"

"Grad student," I said. My heart started to palpitate. I thought he was cute.

"You look younger," Steve said with an endearing smile. I felt myself weaken, a genuine surprise considering my emotions were so tightly wound.

Although I had planned to stay for an hour, two quickly passed while I talked to Steve. Beyond the usual pleasantries, we shared bits and pieces of our lives. He was a teaching assistant at the university, eager to secure a full-time job as a graphic artist. He showed no reaction when I said I was an orphan. The party was in full swing and Steve asked,

"Would you like to have coffee or something?"

"No thanks, I was thinking of leaving. I have to work in the morning."

Acting the perfect gentleman, he asked, "May I escort you home?"

A warm feeling fluttered in my stomach. "Sure, that would be nice."

On the drive home, I caught Steve's eyes checking me out. I wondered if he had dated black women before or if I was his first. I hated being the first. Whites who befriended or dated blacks frequently asked inane questions, such as, "Is your pubic hair tightly curled?" or "Do you like fried chicken?"

In front of my house, Steve stopped the car and said, "May I see you again?"

"Yes." He leaned over to kiss me, but I ducked out of the car. I could only handle so much.

We started dating right away. For once, I felt like everyone else. I had a boyfriend. Steve paid attention to me, and I soaked up the affection like a withering plant drinking in water. At least he was not after my money. I had nothing but a mountain of college loans hanging over me, and no tangible assets.

Things moved so fast that I didn't really learn to know him very well. If Steve had a favorite color or liked classical music, I had no idea. Looking back, I wonder if I was replaying the fleeting relationships of foster care by getting involved with someone I barely knew.

In early May 1977, only a few months after

we'd met, Steve accepted a job in Sacramento at a whopping salary of $18,500. I wondered what would become of our whirlwind romance. It seemed over so soon.

Over dinner the next night, Steve said, "I'd like you to join me in California."

A twitter jolted my stomach. "Really?"

"Is that a yes or a no?"

I had no family to run this by for approval. I hadn't kept in touch with the few friends I had from Buffalo. I thought about calling Jeanne but decided not to. She would not approve because I barely knew Steve. But I accepted his offer anyway. "I'd love to, but I have to take exams and finish my degree."

He said he understood.

I was so smitten by his affection that I ignored my common sense. The smart move would have been to go slowly, to test the waters, but I plunged right in. I had no idea if Steve and I were compatible.

By midnight on graduation day, I sat in my room, still clad in a cap and gown. Steve hadn't called to congratulate me, nor had he sent a card. What I did receive was a ticket for an economy airline in a plain envelope imprinted with his name and address. He had traveled first class but said money was tight, so did I mind flying on a start-up airline? I should have stayed put, but I acted with my heart, not my mind. It would be a long time before I found my way out of this tunnel.

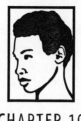

CHAPTER 10

Till Death Do Us Part?

Steve met me at the crowded Sacramento airport. Beard trimmed and hair cut short, he sported khaki slacks with a sharp, scissors-like crease, a crisp button-down cotton shirt, and shiny, tasseled loafers. Considering he claimed to live on a budget, he resembled a Wall Street investment banker on his day off. To launch his career, new clothes were certainly needed, but his outfit appeared top of the line. Had he robbed a bank before he went shopping?

"Hi," he said, with a halfhearted hug. "I missed you."

"I missed you, too." In my confused way, I had.

Once we exchanged hugs and kisses, I said, "We need the luggage area so I can pick up my suitcase."

The long trip had exhausted me, and I wanted sleep. A bit of courtesy would have been nice, but Steve did not offer to carry my bag as we threaded our way through swarms of passengers. He talked about the latest sports gossip. Who cared? I was tired, hungry, and not interested in a lecture on sports figures.

Prior to my arrival, Steve had rented a five-room apartment in a somewhat shabby brick building. The surrounding neighborhood seemed tolerable. At least there were no gangs and hookers plying their trades on street corners. The 1950s-style railroad apartment had not been renovated or painted, but for the time being it was home.

Steve slid out of his jacket and fussed with the hanger before finally closing the hall closet. He found me in the bathroom where I was splashing water on my face. Caressing me by the waist, he gently turned me around and pressed his body against mine. Although my mouth tasted like sand, he kissed me and said, "I've thought about you all day."

I was far from in the mood, but I gave in to his wishes. We climbed into bed. As soon as he was finished, he pulled on his boxer shorts and hopped out of bed. My satisfaction seemed not to matter. Was this why he missed me?

"I'm going to watch the A's game," Steve said. "I'll be in later."

After eating a few slices of pizza alone, I showered and changed into my pajamas. I lay in bed, feeling flustered and uncertain. Suddenly I was sharing my life with a man I hardly knew. In all the years since I left foster care, not much had changed. I was still allowing strangers to rule my life. Was this a pattern I could ever unlearn?

By the time I woke up the next morning, Steve was gone. I assumed he had gone for breakfast. I hoped he would bring something back for me. There was nothing edible in the house besides a pack of hard peppermint candy and stale Ritz crackers.

While I dressed, he returned with fresh bagels and a container of orange juice. Over breakfast, we talked about his new job.

"I work with *such* assholes," he said.

"The whole company or just a few people in your department?"

Heaping cream cheese on his bagel, he took a bite and said, "Half of them never read a newspaper or watch the news. They don't know anything about the nuclear arms race with the Soviet Union. The girls are into disco and *Saturday Night Fever*. With co-workers like them, I'll be vice president within a year." In a short time, his ego had ballooned to the size of a Cadillac.

"Girls? If someone is old enough to work at your company, isn't she a woman?"

Ignoring my remark, he glanced at his watch and said, "Look at the time already. The game is on. I hope I didn't miss anything." He planted himself in front of the wobbly black and white television set and turned it on. He seemed to have forgotten my existence. Didn't he wonder if I had plans for the day, knowing I was new to the area and didn't know my way around? Had I felt better about myself, I would not have let his indifference slip by.

His preoccupation with sports told me he was in no big hurry to ask the landlord, who lived downstairs, to repair the broken stove. It had not worked for the three months Steve lived there. Just as well. I lacked culinary skills anyway.

Water stains yellowed the bathroom ceiling. Nests of cockroaches crawled around the kitchen, making me lose my appetite whenever I went in there. No wonder he had squandered so much money on eating out. As a foster child, I had lived in plenty of homes overrun by bugs. I did not relish living with them again. Before I did anything else, I planned to buy roach motels, so our guests would have a place of their own.

Out of the blue one day, Steve said, "I hope the landlord doesn't hassle us because of you."

I looked up in astonishment. "Me? What're you talking about?"

"You know, that you're black. I never told him."

What was I supposed to do about that? I felt as if Steve blamed me for other people's ignorance. "I don't see that as a problem, do you?"

"Oh, all right," he said, blowing my concerns aside. "I'll introduce you to the landlord."

He threw on his shirt and stepped into a pair of shoes.

"Wait, I'll bring coffee and cake," I said sarcastically.

"Don't be smart. This could be serious."

The man's icy stare told me what I already suspected. He barely acknowledged me, but anger raged in his eyes. Steve had to be blind not to notice. Over the next few months, the landlord left us alone, but he glared at me whenever our paths crossed. He also refused to budge about making necessary repairs, so we opted to move.

After driving all over the city, we signed a lease on a two-bedroom apartment in a respectable part of town. Our apartment-shopping was mostly without incident. One landlord, who refused to shake my hand, said he only rented to married couples Did he think I believed his excuse? It didn't matter. The apartment had mice droppings in the kitchen, flecks of paint falling from the living room ceiling, and neighbors who listened to loud, thumping rock music.

Because Steve spent so much money on his wardrobe, our furnishings had to come from the Salvation Army and other thrift stores. We bought a lumpy sofa missing one cushion, along with two cracked end tables. The Formica kitchen table and vinyl chairs were circa 1950s. So were the two-drawer desk, bookcase, and bedroom dresser. The manager contributed a throw rug that looked ready for the trash heap. We splurged, however, on a brand new queen-size bed. The place was barely OK, but we made do.

Now that we had a place to live, I concentrated on employment. Steve's salary covered our bills, except for my student loans. The bank offered new graduates a six-month grace period. Mine was about to expire. Soon they would be breathing down my neck for repayment.

I typed my resume and made copies at the public library. I expected my educational background to protect me from the bleakness of the unemployment line. It did not. Some job applications were met with rejection letters. Others were ignored. I tried to remain upbeat, but the negative responses that arrived daily stung me with depression. If I had so much trouble landing a job, I could barely imagine the disappointment my less-educated brothers and sisters felt as they pounded the pavement searching for a paycheck.

Some days I felt too discouraged to answer want ads. I cringed at the idea of working in a grocery store again, but with loan payments hanging over my head that became a real possibility.

I felt some relief knowing Jeff and Lauren lived reasonably close by. They had married and moved to San Francisco the year before. Although Steve and I lived on a tight budget, I managed a call to Lauren now and then. I missed spending time with them, especially Lauren. We had enjoyed many long talks together. They wanted to meet Steve and we agreed to get together soon. Because I had so much trouble maintaining friendships, I let most of them slip away. There were people from Buffalo I regretted blowing off. I hoped I could keep up the friendship with Jeff and Lauren.

As our finances dwindled so did our dinner choices. At a meal of boiled potatoes and frozen peas, Steve asked, "Did you find a job today?"

He never showed a glimmer of understanding about my dilemma.

I picked at my food. "Nothing yet."

"What about your student loans? Because of you, I was late paying the phone bill."

"Steve, I leave the house before you every morning. I make calls, I drop off resumes, and I check out the want ads."

"If you don't find a job soon, we might have to eat TV dinners. God, I hate TV dinners."

"Did you hear me? I said I was trying. What more do you want from me?"

Ignoring my frustration, he said, "The A's won last night."

"So what?"

"Jesus Christ, don't take it out on me," he said, flinging his napkin on the floor.

Bottled up anger caused me to grip my fork. "I'll find a job soon." I felt like poking his rear end with it.

We finished dinner in chilly silence. Later that night, I lay in bed staring at the ceiling. I felt scared and alone. When Steve rolled over and took off his underwear, I pretended interest. I wonder if he noticed?

It took almost six months to secure a full-time job at a community development organization at a lofty salary of $800 per month, without benefits. My self-esteem was saved, thank goodness, and for a while Steve stopped hassling me about money.

As weeks passed, I felt as isolated with Steve as I did in foster care. With few friends or family connections, we spent a great deal of time with each other. Even then, we barely interacted. Conversations were strained. In most ways, we were strangers. This man was my boyfriend, yet I forced myself to like him. Was this what a romantic relationship was supposed to be like? Where were the long-stemmed roses, the boxes of sweet milk chocolates, and the mushy cards? *Maybe that came later,* I thought.

Demand on our income exceeded our supply, so options for entertainment were limited as well. We took long walks through city parks and hiking trails. Occasionally, we treated ourselves to dinner and a movie. Now and then, we ventured to a local museum or historical site. We tried to act civil towards one another.

One evening after dinner, Steve asked, "Do you want to get married?"

I almost choked on a bite of potato salad. "Married?"

"Yes," he said, as he took my hand, "married."

I wondered what prompted him to ask.

"What will your parents say?" I had never met either of his parents, who were divorced. I suspected they knew little if anything about me, especially not my race.

"I hope they'll be happy for me," he said.

"And if they're not?"

"Let me handle them."

Foolish as it was, I said yes. Why? Saying yes to Steve was another in a long line of incidents where I handed my fate over to someone else. As a child, I hadn't had a choice; all decisions were out of my hands. As an adult, I had choices—but I didn't know how to make them. Or dare to make them. Except for a co-worker with whom I maintained a cordial relationship, I told no one the good news. But was it really good news? I felt as listless as a quart of milk sitting in a crate.

As expected, his divorced parents went ballistic. His mother slammed down the phone when Steve broke the news. Then she called back to berate Steve and insist that an interracial marriage interfered with God's wishes. If he carried through his plans, she warned, their relationship would end. And for a while, it did.

For a man who was born and raised in California, his father Joe spit fire like an old cracker from the worst Jim Crow days of the South. "If you marry my son, I'll kill you," he shouted at me on the phone one night.

"Steve proposed to *me*," I said, somehow maintaining my composure.

"My son has bad judgment. Leave him. Now."

"Sir, I think Steve needs to decide for himself," I said. Butting heads with this old mule was not easy.

"He doesn't need to be messing with *you people*." Joe's rage made him sound like he was foaming at the mouth. "Stay away from him. And Jesus Christ, I hope you're not pregnant. For crying out loud, I don't want a mulatto grandchild."

I hadn't expected to be welcomed with open arms, but their extreme reaction stunned me. How would Steve respond? Perhaps it was best we called off the wedding. Nothing seemed to fit anyway.

But we didn't. In a civil ceremony with no one present, we married in November 1977. No one threw rice or showered us with gifts and cash. I did not have the customary walk down the aisle while the organist played "Here Comes the Bride," or the chance to throw my bouquet to an eager group of hopeful women. The Peggy Lee song, "Is That All There Is?" came to mind.

At least my teeth benefited from marriage. Steve's job provided me with medical and dental benefits. The last time I'd had health coverage was in the early 1970s when I was still a foster child covered by Medicaid. I promptly saw a dentist and spent several hundred dollars correcting my badly neglected teeth. I also had a thorough medical check-up. With the exception of an ingrown toenail, I was pronounced in good health. As for my mental health, that was another story.

*   *   *

An avid sports fan, Steve spent most of his free time watching baseball, football, or basketball. I did not share his enthusiasm for the Oakland As, the San Francisco Forty-Niners, or the San Francisco Giants. So while he parked himself in front of the TV set, I entertained myself. Mostly I took long walks or spent time in the library. On Sunday mornings, I usually noshed on bagels in a nearby cafe and read the newspaper. Weekend afternoons were reserved for housekeeping. Dusty furniture and piles of dirty clothes did not faze Steve. Housework, he said, was beneath him, yet we could not afford a maid. I balked at living in a pigsty, so I tidied the apartment myself. I considered myself calm and peaceful, but at times I felt like swatting him with the broom.

Late on a Sunday afternoon while I swept the floors, Steve started hugging and kissing me.

"Steve, I'm trying to clean," I said, pushing him away.

He stroked the back of my neck. "The heck with the floors."

"Later," I said, "when I'm done."

Steve persisted and as usual, I went along. Our sex life was largely perfunctory, sort of like making a tuna sandwich. I could take or leave intimacy with Steve. Once he had finished, he went back to the TV. I stopped expecting or wanting more.

About six months after we married, Steve mentioned an upcoming office dinner party at his supervisor's house. "People who want to get ahead have to attend these things."

"What day is it and what should I wear?" I asked. I didn't relish the idea of socializing with Steve's co-workers, but I assumed it was my wifely duty to attend.

"It's next Saturday," he said. A not-so-funny look dimmed his eyes. "But you can't go."

"Why, is it only for employees?"

"Not really," he said, stammering. "I . . . I . . . I . . . ."

"What's the problem?" I asked.

"I didn't tell anyone my wife was black."

That was a low blow I did not expect. My own husband was ashamed of me. I turned aside, so he would not know I was hurt.

"Were you ever going to tell them?" I asked. "Or did you plan to invite Angela Davis over to make the announcement?"

"Don't be mad," he said. "You don't understand. If I get this promotion, it'll mean more money for both of us."

He was right. How could I understand? I retreated to the other room, humiliated that my husband had so little respect for me.

Steve followed me, but I turned away. "Don't touch me."

"I'm sorry," he said. "How can I make it up to you?"

I grabbed my jacket, slammed the door, and walked for the next two hours. When I came home, neither of us broached the subject. I was a fool to let it pass, but I did. Had I been stronger, I would have shown more self-respect, but emotionally I was still a lonely child.

Steve was firmly in charge of our lives. He made up the shopping list, planned our meals, and decided what movies we would see. My skin color had cost him a relationship with his parents, as well as some friends. He said he did not care, but I couldn't believe that was true. My guilt contributed to the way I caved in to his demands.

Gradually, I developed a friendship with Carl, a black man at my office who had recently won sole custody of his six-year-old son. His wife had walked out without notice. Tender and loving, Carl clearly doted on his son. I admired his steadfast devotion to his only child. Once, I mentioned him to Steve, who immediately stiffened.

"Oh," he said. There was a sudden chill in his voice.

"He's been a good friend," I said. "He talks about his son every day. I'd like to invite them over for dinner sometime."

"Why, so you can show off your new romance in my face?"

"What?? That's ridiculous! Carl and I are just friends," I said, surprised and disappointed. "Steve, I need a friend, and that's all Carl is. He's been through a lot, and he needs someone to talk to."

"I won't shake hands with a man trying to steal my wife." He backed away from me like I was rabid. "No, not me."

I was so frustrated. Defending my platonic relationship with an officemate seemed fruitless, so I changed the subject. Sighing, I said, "Do you feel like going out for dinner?"

"The game is on," he said with a sour expression. "I can't leave now, I could miss something."

"I'm going out then. See you later."

"Tell Carl I said hello." Sarcasm filled his voice. "I always wondered when you'd look for dark meat." He let out a nasty laugh.

"You're not funny," I said as I headed out the door.

My friendship with Lauren grew as much as I could allow it to. I think she understood my odd nature, because she was always careful how far she probed. As fond as I was of both Jeff and Lauren, I still hid my inner feelings.

One afternoon when Lauren called, she said, "Girl, I've got the greatest news. Ready for this? I'm pregnant."

I yearned for a rock-solid relationship like she had with Jeff. I envied the closeness Lauren shared with her husband. It was clear to me that Steve and I would never be close. I knew part of that was my fault. I grew up without trust. That was an aspect of my personality that I couldn't seem to change.

"That's great news," I said. "When are you due?"

"I'm 26 weeks. I'm huge already. I don't know how I'll carry this baby for nine months."

"You and Jeff will make terrific parents," I said,

wondering if I ever would.

"I hope so. Hey, how are you and Steve getting along?"

"OK, I guess," I said.

"Girl, don't bullshit me."

I told her about our escalating problems with his parents, our inability to communicate, and our frequent bickering. I was trapped inside a loveless marriage. As unhappy as I was, I feared being miserable on my own. The idea of meeting another man terrified me.

"Have you thought about a separation?"

"Not yet," I said. "It's just such a hard choice to make."

"Have you and Steve talked about it?" Lauren asked.

"No."

"Maybe you should."

"I can't," I said.

We vowed to keep in touch.

As a child, the holidays sent me tumbling in the dumps. New York State provided Catholic Charities with barely enough funding to cover foster children's food, clothing, and medical care, so nothing was left for Christmas gifts. My foster parents, all of whom came from modest backgrounds, squeezed a few extra dollars from their own budgets to buy at least one present, usually a scarf or a pair of mittens, for us foster children. Since my January birthday was so close to Christmas, that was rarely celebrated.

Holiday seasons during my marriage felt as bleak as those of my childhood. I forced myself to be pleasant when I felt like crying. I went Christmas shopping when I felt like sleeping. I decorated a tree when I felt like hiding in a closet. I excelled at pretending I was full of joy to the world when I was really living a silent night.

Oddly enough, Steve and I collected unique, hand-made Christmas ornaments over the years. So when the yuletide season rolled around and we put up a tree, at least I had distinctive ornaments to look at. I tried to persuade myself that that made for a happy holiday, but I was shielding myself from the cold reality of our existence.

Because we rarely made friends, we stayed home most holidays and did nothing special. During our seven years together, we may have spent one or two holidays with Jeff and Lauren. Generally, to me, Christmas and Thanksgiving were just like any other day.

As a child I was always kept out of the kitchen except at mealtimes. Never having learned to cook, I grew up as the queen of packaged foods. I rarely turned down a dinner invitation. When friends talked about cooking their favorite dishes, I joked that I made a good guest. The art of preparing a lavish holiday meal takes both organizational skills, a sense of timing, and cooking talent. Neither my husband nor I possessed such gifts, so we generally ate a perfunctory dinner at a local restaurant. I was always relieved when January arrived.

One holiday season, however, was unusually

warm and pleasant. Steve surprised me with reservations at a rustic lodge in Yosemite National Park. On Christmas day, we enjoyed a seven-course dinner. Afterwards, we went ice-skating and hiking. I have two left feet, so I opted not to join Steve for a skiing adventure down the slopes. That evening, we sat around the fireplace in the communal room of the lodge. He sipped hot chocolate, while I had hot cider with a stick of cinnamon. We chatted with other guests, who had come from all over the U.S. and abroad. The huge park was utterly magnificent. I had never enjoyed such spectacular scenery. I was sorry the three-day trip ended so soon. The trip was the highlight of our marriage. We fell back into our unhappy patterns when we returned home.

True to her word, Steve's mother refused to call or write. His father's ever-present threats and rage, however, made up for her absence. He remained a persistent nuisance, calling us frequently, always uttering profanities. I was glad he lived over 100 miles away.

One night Steve worked late. The phone rang so I picked up the receiver. I should have let it ring.

"What the hell are you still doing there?" Joe barked, grilling me like a hard-nosed detective.

"I live here," I said, hands shaking. Although he was far away, his anger hit me like a fist in the face.

"Get out," he thundered.

"Sir, Steve and I are married."

"Jesus Christ, not if I can help it."

I hung up the phone. Joe called back, but I refused to answer. The phone rang for so long I picked up and left the receiver off the hook.

When Steve came home, he asked, "Why is the phone off the hook?"

"Your father called and told me to get out."

Sighing, Steve said, "I wish he wouldn't do that."

"Talk to him. He scares me."

"Yeah, all right." His apathy was impossible. "I'll call tomorrow."

"I'm really afraid of him," I said.

Steve made a face as if I had over-reacted. "My old man? That weasel?"

"That weasel hasn't threatened you, just me."

Steve must have taken notice of my shaky voice because he held me and said, "I'll protect you."

I wondered if he would. Or could.

At dinner, Steve usually browsed through the daily newspaper. Once he asked, "What do you think of the *Mary Tyler Moore Show*?"

I had not given it much thought. "Why?"

"Just wanted your opinion," he said as if I was a participant in a survey. "What about *Rhoda*?"

"Steve, I'm not a TV fan," I said, puzzled why he had not noticed in all that time.

"Oh yeah, that's right. Maybe we should spend more time together," he said. Pushing back on his chair, he got up and left the table. I heard the roar of fans at a football game, so I went to bed.

Persistent depression picked apart my soul. Almost every day I woke up feeling disconnected to people, including my husband, places, and things. On the other hand, he seemed just as disconnected to me. Did he see me as his wife, or as some poor black girl who needed to be saved?

But that was exactly how I saw myself. While most children had families to look after them, I relied on myself. While many decisions were out of my hands, such as where I lived or with whom, I was forced to care for myself emotionally. I made tough decisions no child should have to make. By adolescence I lived independently. I may have been only a teen, but I behaved as an adult. A part of me longed to be cared for. Years later, I recognized how I lived out this fantasy in my marriage. I wasn't prepared for a husband, any more than Steve was prepared for a wife. Whether I knew it or not, I was drawn to the idea of someone re-parenting me, caring for me as I never had been cared for as a child.

To try to block out my unhappiness, I slept more and more. Even if a miracle drug had been available, I doubt I would have taken it. How could I, an allegedly happily married woman, ask for a happy pill?

Home alone one day, I looked around the silent apartment and noticed the near total absence of cozy touches. The white walls were empty—there were no framed posters, family pictures, or colorful paintings. There were no houseplants. Neither of us collected knickknacks. As a child, I never added

homey touches to my rooms. Steve had no flair for decorating, either. So the place looked as boring as a slice of American cheese.

I thought about adopting a dog. During my frequent jaunts through the neighborhood, I met a lot of dog owners out with their four-footed friends. I did not always remember the neighbors' names, but I knew all the local dogs. Every Friday night, a group of dog owners and their pets hung out in a nearby park and chatted for what seemed like hours. I was envious of the camaraderie they shared. Perhaps a dog would add some warmth to our chilly home.

Steve and I had never discussed pet ownership. One evening after dinner I broached the subject. "What would you think about adopting a dog? We could get one from the Sacramento animal shelter."

He acted as if I said adopt a gorilla. "A dog! What's wrong with you? A dog, for Chrissakes."

"I think it'd be nice to have a dog to take out on walks," I said. "Our neighbors have dogs, and they all know each other."

"No way," he said. "I'm not picking up dog crap like those idiots do. And I don't want some goofy dog slobbering all over my face or getting its paw prints on my good clothes. The answer is no."

"But . . ." I wanted him to at least consider it.

Abruptly, he stormed away. I was disappointed. I hoped a furry friend would be the companion Steve was not. That was the only discussion we had or the subject.

*   *   *

If Steve was surprised by my desire for a dog, he surprised me more soon after. One evening he said, "Maybe we should have a baby like your friends."

Caught totally by surprise, I said, "That's not a good idea."

"Why not? What about what I want?"

For lots of reasons, I doubted either of us would make good parents. "My childhood left a big emotional hole in my life. You know the hard time I have expressing my emotions. No Steve, I don't want to have a child."

"You don't like children?" he asked.

"That's not what I said. I wouldn't make a good mother."

"That may be true, but I'd be a good father."

He had a habit of insulting me, and I fell into a pattern of ignoring the stinging jabs.

"I don't plan to stop using birth control," I said. "And then there's your family to deal with. Your father still erupts about our marriage. If he knew I was pregnant, he'd blow up."

Steve touched my cheek. "At least think about having a baby before you say no."

"I've already thought about it," I said, "and the answer is no."

"You're not being fair to me," he said.

"That's how I felt when I asked you about getting a dog."

"I'm talking about a baby, for God sakes, not a mutt."

This time I was the one who walked out of the room. No way did I want to become a mother. I carried so much excess baggage I was sure I would cripple a child emotionally.

*　　*　　*

Joe stepped up the hostile phone calls, regardless of Steve's efforts to quell his father's rage. The incessant ringing caused us to automatically leave the phone off the hook. No one got through.

Finally prevented from spewing forth venom on the phone, Joe resorted to mailing hate-filled letters with language so vile I trembled upon opening them. Steve could no longer make light of his father's fury. The letters made serious threats of bodily harm against both of us. Joe sounded worse than some goombah from the Mafia.

One night, Steve and I were in bed ready to go through the motions of sex. A loud pounding on the door startled us. Both of us instantly knew who it was. We looked at one another and said, "He's here."

"Call the police," I said. "What if he has a gun?"

"Heck, I don't know what he's up to, but I can't get him in trouble. He's my father."

"Joe is causing a lot of trouble for me and you too," I said, shaking like it was 25 below.

"I'll see if I can calm him down," Steve said, throwing on his jeans.

I grabbed his arm. "No, don't go."

"What should we do?"

Our nosy neighbor's intervention saved us. The old biddy had heard the commotion and called her son, who lived downstairs, for help. The young man, built like a tank, interrupted Joe, who was ready to start banging on our door again. I heard him say to Joe, "You got a problem, Mack? Handle it some other way. Either you leave now or I'll bash your face in. And then I'll knock your teeth out. That's just for starters."

Quiet followed. But we were seriously scared. The following morning, Steve and I quit our jobs. We stayed in a motel for a week and then left California. We fled to Oregon, hoping to find safe haven from Joe.

CHAPTER 11

Back and Forth

Perhaps we over-reacted, but Joe frightened us. As a couple of very private people, neither of us wanted to involve the police. Joe's repeated harassment had worn us down. Leaving seemed a natural response.

We had saved enough money to put down a deposit on a one-bedroom apartment in a fairly stable Portland neighborhood. Steve found work within a week of our arrival. His job was on the outskirts of the city, so he needed a car to commute. We stretched our budget enough to buy a used Toyota Corolla.

My job search, however, was not as fruitful. I received so many rejection letters that I had all the standard lines memorized.

"Dear Applicant,

"Due to a hiring freeze, our company is not currently accepting applications. We will keep your application on file should a suitable position open up. We wish you the best of luck."

Who needed luck? I needed a job. The banks wanted their money back.

"Dear Applicant,

"Thank you for your interest in our company. After a thorough interview process, we hired another applicant. Our very best to you in your job search."

Did they have to rub it in by saying they hired someone else? Who cared about their best wishes?

Then there were the much less formalized post-cards: "Unfortunately, we do not have any openings at the present time. Thank you for your interest."

Why did they bother wasting paper and postage? The constant snubs gnawed at my spirit. I had two college degrees from respectable universities, some work experience, and a stack of recommendation letters; still I had trouble landing employment. Was it related to my race or the downturn in the economy? It was probably both. Still, not having a job squashed my already fragile self-esteem. Steve, who was never unemployed for more than a few weeks, had trouble relating to my anguish.

Late one afternoon, he found me in bed. I had no interviews scheduled, so I saw no need to shower or dress. All human beings need to feel productive and to be a part of something. Unemployment weighed down my weary soul. I had all the classic symptoms of depression, yet I never sought help. I was afraid once I got on the therapist's couch I would never get off it again.

Flipping on the bedroom light, Steve asked, "Are you sick or something?"

I barely rolled over. "No."

Should I have told him about the recurring dream plaguing me? I received a phone call asking me to come for an interview. I showered, dressed, and showed up promptly at the manager's office. Always, there was a long line of people. Every time my turn arrived, the person in charge of hiring burst out laughing, then disappeared. I woke up frightened I would never find a job.

Steve now stood over me acting more annoyed than concerned. "What's wrong then?"

"I didn't feel like getting up."

"Why not?"

I tossed off the covers and said, "I don't have a job. I didn't even have any interviews scheduled. So why should I get up?"

"Everyone gets up."

"Leave me alone," I said. My mouth tasted like grit, a reminder my teeth needed brushing. Steve was still in the room, so I curled under the blanket. I refused to budge.

"Fine, stay here then. I'm going out for dinner."

Several minutes later, the door slammed, and I closed my eyes. I had stopped caring what he thought. If I wanted to sink further into a depression, he could not stop me.

*　　　*　　　*

Of course, we fretted about the bills, especially our student loans that plowed us under in debt. At the breakfast table one day Steve asked, "Have you applied for a deferral yet?"

"I did, but they want me to either register with an employment agency or with my school. That doesn't help because I didn't graduate from any local schools and most city planning jobs aren't handled by employment agencies."

"What happened when you told them?" he asked.

"Nothing. They sent me another form letter saying the exact same thing: 'Register with your school or employment agency.'"

"Stubborn bastards, aren't they?" he said. "What are we going to do?" His eyes twitched.

I sensed he was nervous about making our monthly obligations. I was, too.

"I don't know," I said, smacked by guilt.

"They're hiring at the grocery store," he said as if talking to a high school student looking for a first job.

"Are we that bad off?" I asked. I dreaded the idea of menial employment, but our survival might depend on it. "If I have to, I will."

"You might," he said. "It won't be that bad."

"How do you know?"

I felt even more demoralized because he failed to acknowledge my pain. If he was on the verge of working as a cashier, no doubt he would have bitterly complained about it.

* * *

The empty feelings deepened. That emotional black hole I kept running from seemed only inches away from caving in on me. For a week or so, I quit looking for work. I could not bear another rejection letter. I barely ate, rarely washed, and stopped combing my hair. As my emotional state slid downward, I lost interest in almost everything, including sex. Our intimate life was so tedious; not much Steve did aroused me.

As usual one night, Steve watched a college football game. Bored, I retired early. I woke up to find Steve fondling me. "Steve, not tonight. I'm tired."

"That's what you always say." He pouted like a little boy whose mother said no to an ice cream cone.

"Maybe tomorrow."

"What about my needs? I have feelings too," he said.

"I'm sorry, Steve, but I just can't."

He stormed out of bed and into the bathroom. I heard the pipes rattle, so I surmised he took another cold shower. It was hard to empathize with him since he had so little understanding of my despair. The sad part was I stopped caring.

Out of the blue one morning, I received a call from a semi-private planning agency. It was looking for a temporary planner and invited me for an interview. I had hoped for a permanent position, but considering we were being hampered by past due bills, I went. I left the office with an appointment for a six-month position. That day, for a change, my mood slightly improved.

Our new life in Portland dragged by. Although we had jobs which kept our noses above water financially, we lived like hermits. We had no friends. Only a few neighbors acknowledged us. I always wondered if Steve shied away from people because of my race. I hedged about meeting people because I was so miserable. Who would want to be around me? Mostly, Steve watched television, and I read or took walks. The lack of family ties and friends cut us off from the community. I called Lauren now and then, but with a new baby for her to care for, our conversations were brief.

One evening, we explored our choices. We could stay and make the most of it, just as we had been doing. That option lacked appeal because neither of us was happy in Oregon. The cold, rainy weather further dampened our spirits. I could take or leave my job and so could Steve. Another option was to move to a mutually agreeable city like Seattle. Or we could return to California.

"What about your father?" I asked as we picked at our takeout Chinese food.

"We've talked a few times," Steve said. "He's not going to hurt you."

"Are you sure? I'm not moving back if he'll still make threats against me. Against us." Life was stressful enough without Joe's constant barbs.

"We won't give him our phone number," Steve said. He assured me Joe lived far enough away that a chance encounter would be extremely unlikely.

"What about your mother?"

"I haven't talked to her in over a year, and I doubt she speaks to him. Remember, they've been divorced for at least six years."

The next day, we handed in our resignation letters and started packing. I wanted to believe that another change of scene was what our marriage needed.

A cheap flat over a hardware store in a working-class section of San Francisco became our next home. Steve found a job right away. His salary was enough to keep us afloat until I landed something, which would hopefully be soon.

Not relying solely on the private sector, I took a lengthy civil-service exam and passed. Soon the city of San Francisco hired me as a planner. I had struck gold.

On a lazy Saturday afternoon as Steve watched a football game and I putzed around the house, the phone rang. Steve called out, "I got it."

Telephone calls during game time irked him. He usually let me handle the phone.

"Hi," he said in a lowered voice.

We paid our bills on time, so I doubted it was a collection agency. We had no friends. Those were the days before telemarketers. Who could it have been?

"I didn't think you'd call anymore," Steve said.

The awkward conversation made my ears prick up.

"How did you find my number, Dad?"

Dad? Was this for real? To keep out distracting street noise, I shut the kitchen window, and then sat down to listen to Steve's conversation.

"We moved to get away from you. Your calls were unbearable, and Theresa was afraid you'd hurt her. I wasn't sure what you'd do."

Too bad I could not hear what Joe said.

"Sorry is a little too late at this point, don't you think? You acted like a street thug. For crying out loud, I was embarrassed to say you were my father."

Steve said yes, no, yes, then finally, "OK. I'll meet you for lunch next week, but only lunch. I'll pick the place. I'm not ready to give you my work address."

After he hung up, I approached him and said, "You're meeting him for lunch?"

"I know this must be a surprise, but he's my father. I guess I gave him a second chance," Steve said, averting his eyes.

"Don't tell him where we live," I said.

"You heard everything I said. I didn't tell him anything personal about us."

Steve flicked on the ballgame, so I returned to the kitchen. I hoped he had not made a mistake. This time I vowed to call the police if Joe threatened to hurt me. My safety was more important than Steve's unyielding pride.

*　　　*　　　*

Lauren was delighted when we moved to San Francisco because she and Jeff lived there. They invited us for dinner one evening. They had not yet met Steve. I was excited about seeing their newborn daughter, Lisa. Steve hedged about buying a baby gift, but I insisted. At that crucial time in my life, Jeff and Lauren were the only true friends I had.

After the usual introductions, Steve and I took turns holding Lisa. She was so tiny, with skin as smooth as a rose. She had Lauren's dark skin, Jeff's mahogany eyes, and a headful of wispy curls. She was beautiful.

We talked a bit while Jeff finished cooking dinner. Steve responded to Lauren's questions about work and family with stiff courtesy, but he kept fiddling with his tie. He checked his watch at least three times. I wondered if he was uncomfortable around more than one black person?

Over a dinner of roasted chicken breasts, rice pilaf, and tossed green salad, Lauren asked Steve to pass the garlic bread. The wicker breadbasket was closest to him.

"Hey Theresa, give her the bread," Steve said as he sliced his chicken.

Lauren's eyes nearly shot out of her head. Unlike me, however, she took none of his crap. "Steve, I asked *you* to pass the bread."

I could tell from the way his eyes narrowed that he was pissed off. He picked up the breadbasket and handed it to Lauren. The two exchanged an uneasy glance. I worried about the rest of the meal.

"Jeff, tell them about your job interview in Cincinnati," Lauren said.

"I hope to get an offer soon," Jeff said, "as an associate professor. It'll be a step up from my current position. We could also use the extra money now that we have Lisa."

"You're lucky they have those affirmative action things," Steve said with a nervous laugh.

Jeff's smile faded. Lauren and I looked at one another and rolled our eyes around.

"If I get this job it'll be due to my qualifications, not my skin color," Jeff said. He gazed directly at Steve.

Steve must have realized he was on the spot because he made no more smart remarks.

Lauren heard Lisa's cries and asked me to help change the baby's diaper. I left Steve alone with Jeff in the kitchen.

Quickly, Lauren shut the bedroom door. "Girl, how do you put up with that jackass?"

I shrugged. "I don't know."

"You can do a lot better. Find someone who treats you with respect. Show his sorry ass the door. Wait, I'll go open it."

"I guess I'm not ready to be alone."

"I'd put his behind out in a snap," Lauren said as she threw the soiled diaper away. "Don't let him treat you like that."

We left without having dessert.

*　　　*　　　*

Steve and I both worked downtown, so we rode the subway every day. We held onto our aging car, even though it had close to 100,000 miles on it. A nearby parking garage with affordable rates offered long-term parking, so we stored the car there. We had over $20,000 in the bank. I felt like we were rich.

One evening, Steve mulled over our money and tax returns. He said, "Let's buy a house. We're getting killed on taxes."

"Can we afford one?"

"I think so. Besides, we need a tax deduction."

A realtor drove us around and around until we settled on a two-family house across the San Francisco Bay in Mill Valley, a quaint city with narrow streets, stylish wood frame homes, and a real downtown. I was shocked by the $120,000 price tag. I was not sure we could afford it, but the bank lent us the money. After closing the deal, we refurbished the downstairs apartment and advertised it as a rental. The extra income would help meet our mortgage payment.

Owning a home was a dream beyond imagining for a poor, orphaned black girl from the ghetto. For my first 19 years I lived in substandard houses, some infested with vermin, others violating building codes, and one that was an absolute pigsty. Although our new home needed work, to me it was like a mansion.

The surprise call came while I was at work. Steve said, "My dad wants to help refinish the house."

My heart sank. "I'm going to a motel. Call me

when it's done."

"He's changed," Steve, said, "give him a chance."

"What, to use me as target practice?"

"If Joe does the work, it'll save us money."

We were no longer desperate. "Steve, I said no."

Steve badgered me for so long I relented. But I said, "I refuse to be in the house when Joe's there. Give me a schedule, so I know how long to stay out. And make sure he doesn't plant any booby traps for me."

Steve accepted his father's offer to help fix up the house. I stayed away whenever acid mouth was around. Over time, Steve and his father repaired their damaged relationship. Father and son went out to dinner, ball games, and met for drinks at a local pub. As time passed, I relaxed my refusal to see Joe. I maintained a phony civil relationship with Joe when I agreed to spend time with him.

One of those rare occasions was the following December 25th. Steve accepted a dinner invitation to spend the holiday with his father and his new bride. I forced myself to smile when Steve introduced me to his stepmother. I wondered if his father saw through my fake expression? The day went along without a hitch until we exchanged gifts. Joe handed me a package that looked messily wrapped, as though it had been done at the last minute. I pretended not to notice. When I opened it, I felt humiliated. Joe had given his son and his wife thoughtful gifts, while I received a cheap pair of gloves that had obviously already been worn. I suppose they belonged to his wife. I felt Steve's eyes boring into me. I hoped he was not expecting me to show gratitude, because there was no way I could say thank you. I put down the box and excused myself. On our way out, I didn't bother asking for my present. Joe called Steve later that night to say I forgot my gift.

A renovated house with a tenant who paid rent failed to uplift our sagging marriage. We argued almost daily. I changed my work hours from a day shift to evening hours. I wanted to steer clear of Steve.

Avoidance did not work either. We bickered about everything, including the poor quality of city water. Out of desperation, I said, "We should see a therapist."

"Maybe you're right."

I was surprised he so readily agreed. I offered to set up an appointment.

Therapy hit the magic button, at least for me. Almost immediately, I felt a rapport with Sherry, our therapist, but Steve scoffed at her.

"Why don't you like her?" I asked one morning over breakfast.

"I don't know," he said, grimacing as if he had sat on a rusty nail.

"There must be a reason," I said. She was white, so he couldn't say Sherry sided with me because of race.

"Therapy is absolute bullshit," he said.

"You agreed to try," I said.

"Don't remind me. I made a mistake. You caught me at a weak moment."

Therapy sessions were emotionally raucous. Torrents of pent-up feelings spilled out. Sweeping our problems under the rug all those years had not made them go away. They had grown and festered.

During one particularly draining session, Steve said, "I try so hard with her. I don't know what she wants."

Sherry asked, "Do you ever ask?"

Arms wrapped tightly around his chest, Steve grimaced. Without responding, he snapped his head to the side.

"Was that a yes or a no?" Sherry asked.

"What's this? Gang up on Steve day?"

Edging closer, I said, "When I try to talk to you, the television set is always on. I'm tired of competing with football or baseball for your attention."

"I can say the same about you. I ask for a little sex and you're tired," he said, ramming his fist hard against the couch. His voice rose. "Or you have a headache."

"Steve, calm down," Sherry said. "Therapy is a place to vent our feelings, but I expect my patients to control themselves. You came to me for help, and I'm trying to help you."

Steve jumped up. "I've had enough. I'm out of here. Stay if you want."

I did. I stayed for the remainder of our one-hour session. That night, Steve again told me therapy was horse crap, and he refused to attend another session. For me, however, therapy gave me hope. Week after week, I returned. My sessions with Sherry gave me the sense I was gaining control over my life. I had not felt that way in ages.

During a subsequent session, Sherry asked me, "Why do you stay with Steve if you're so unhappy?"

I was stumped. "I don't know."

"From what you've said and what I heard from him during the few times he was here, it doesn't sound like you two are the least bit compatible."

That was absolutely true.

"Tell me what you are thinking," Sherry said.

I hemmed and hawed until I finally said, "I'm afraid of being alone again. I don't know if I can take that. What should I do?"

"I can't make your decisions. You have to do that. I'm here to help you figure out what's best for you."

"It's so hard to decide anything now."

"You don't have to, but we should keep talking."

I returned again and again, yet I made no move to leave the marriage. Steve grumbled I was wasting our money. He badgered me about what I talked about in therapy. I refused to say. I asked him to rejoin me for sessions, but he said no. He claimed therapy was only for fruitcakes, and that I was the one with the problem.

One day, I woke up in agony from menstrual cramps. For years, I endured bouts of monthly cramps, but usually a few aspirin calmed the pain. This time was different. I took aspirin, drank hot tea, and covered my abdomen with a heating pad, but nothing helped. I even missed a few days at work. Steve said it was probably nothing, and I should not waste our money on a doctor's visit. After several weeks of severe bleeding and killer cramps, I made an appointment anyway. A series of blood and lab tests confirmed the diagnosis of endometriosis, which I learned meant that tissue normally found in the lining of the uterus was growing in other areas. The doctor recommended a hysterectomy—the surgical removal of my uterus. I saw another doctor for a second opinion; the recommendation was the same.

Later that evening, I told Steve the news. "I'll need to have a hysterectomy next week. The doctor said I should be in the hospital for a few days."

"So you want me to drive you?" He acted like I had interrupted something important.

"Yes," I said.

I regretted asking him. We had problems, but after nearly seven years of marriage, I had expected at least some expression of concern. So much for hoping.

*　　　*　　　*

The surgery went well. Steve showed up for a 15-minute visit on the day of the surgery. He came in complaining. "Hospitals make me sick. I don't like the smells."

"Do you want to know how the surgery went?"

"Oh yeah, how are you feeling?"

"I'll be here for three days."

"I can't stay long. You understand, right?"

Steve left while I dozed off. My bed had a telephone available, but I never called home. I figured we would only fight. I was in enough physical pain. Getting into a spat with him would not help me heal. On the day of my discharge, I flagged a taxi and went home.

When the cab pulled up in front of our house, I noticed the car was gone. It was slightly after noon on a weekday. Steve never drove to work. A sinking feeling jostled my stomach. My hands started to sweat. I opened the front door. The place felt emptier than usual. I tripped over myself to reach the bedroom. I checked the closet. Steve's clothes were gone. So were his personal papers. More importantly, so was our bankbook.

I was exhausted and sore from the surgery, but I rifled through the yellow pages until I found our bank's telephone number. I could not remember the account number, but a sympathetic clerk helped me anyway. Then came the bad news. The account had been closed three days earlier, the day of my surgery.

"How can that happen?" I said. Panic choked my voice. I could hardly speak. "We had a joint account. That means he closed the account without my signature."

"Hold on," she said, "let me check."

My hands shook. My knees wobbled. How could he stoop that low?

"I checked the withdrawal slip. Your signature is on it."

"It was forged. I was in the hospital. I can prove it."

"Lady, I'm sorry. There's nothing else I can do. You'd better hire a lawyer."

The receiver slipped out of my hands. I buried my face inside my palms, and for the first time in years, I sobbed. I had no money and no way of paying our mortgage.

I bounced between intense rage and overwhelming sadness. When feeling angry, I tried finding Steve. I wanted him to know how hurt I was. For survival, I wanted half the money back. And then I wanted to see him, so I could smash his face with a hammer. Out of desperation, I called his father Joe, who claimed ignorance. No doubt he lied. I had no way to track down his mother since she had remarried, and I did not know her last name. So I called his workplace.

"Steve, please," I said, trying to sound casual when deep down I felt like cursing. I squeezed an orange pretending it was his head.

"No can do. He quit," the receptionist said. I heard typewriter keys pounding away in the background.

"Wait, don't hang up. I'm his wife and it's important I talk to him."

"What'd he do? Stiff you with the bills? My ex did that, miserable slime that he was. Lady, take my advice and get a private investigator. But let me see what I can find out about Stevie boy."

I gripped the phone so hard my hand hurt. While on hold, I rehearsed what I would say to him. So many thoughts came to mind. Where would I start?

The receptionist came back on the line and said, "Lover boy walked out without a forwarding address."

I was flabbergasted. Everything in my life had changed so suddenly. I was not prepared for this.

"Does anyone know where he went?"

"Wait a sec, I'll ask," she said.

"Nobody knows. Steve wasn't the most popular guy around here. I don't think anybody cares, either. The boss is calling, so I have to go. Find an investigator. Don't let the scumbag screw you. Try to screw him first."

Once I stopped crying, washed my face with cool water, and drank a cup of hot tea, I took an inventory of the house. Not only had Steve emptied our bank account, he had taken all of the decent furniture. All that remained were a few pieces a thrift store might reject. I rummaged through the closets and noticed he helped himself to the Christmas ornaments we had collected. I vowed to never again attach memories to curios, no matter how unusual those items might be. Gone also was our photo album, including the pictures from our wedding. Some women in my position might have burned the wedding album, but for me, who had not even one childhood picture, the loss of even those photos was devastating.

Steve's abandonment and the loss of my savings plunged me deeply into depression. Over the next few months I saw Sherry a few times, but unable to afford a therapist's bills, I soon stopped. Finding it impossible to concentrate, I made a slew of mistakes at work. I bungled reports, missed important meetings, and called in sick at least once a week. Not surprisingly, I was terminated.

My psychological condition deteriorated. I rarely changed clothes. I didn't bathe or comb my hair. I didn't clean the house. Our tenant had moved out, so I had no income at all. For food, I traveled into San Francisco to eat at a soup kitchen. I started praying again and, once in a while, attended church. I was terrified.

The bank eventually repossessed the house. I lost everything. I left what was once my dream house with my clothes inside a brown paper bag, the same way I traveled from one foster home to the next. I was a 27-year-old vagabond. This time I was on my own. The system was not around to protect me, and my life had spiraled out of control.

CHAPTER 12

Boston Yet Again

The year was 1984. Several months of my life remain hazy after I lost my home, my job, and my husband. Seeing the sign nailed on the door ordering me to vacate the premises within 24 hours seared my soul. Losing the house was like being in foster care all over again, except this time there was no caseworker to drag me to another strange family. I was on my own.

I slept in the old car that Steve left behind. I parked in affluent neighborhoods where I felt safe. I hoped my skin color wouldn't draw unwanted attention from the police. To conserve gas, I left the car and walked around. I spent a lot of time sitting on park benches. Feeling grungy from not bathing or brushing my teeth, I hesitated about asking my friends Lauren and Jeff for help, but finally did.

They invited me to stay with them, and I accepted their offer. But as they were expecting their second child and had plans to move to Ohio before long, we all knew that the arrangement was only temporary. I'd have to figure something out soon.

As a way to scrape by and not sponge off my friends, I sold everything, including my prized tool collection. Over the years, I had collected an array of antique tools that I had used for a boat-building course I took. That was one of my dreams—to build a sailboat. I suppose that dream was inspired by those afternoons I'd spent watching the rowing crews on the Charles River back in Boston. I cringed at parting with the tools, but I had no other choice. I desperately needed the money.

I picked up whatever odd jobs I could. I was not in a frame of mind for steady employment. Plus, I was still recovering from a serious operation. My physical, as well as emotional, health was shaky.

Making matters worse, Steve had stuck me with hefty credit card bills. We shared joint accounts, and he ran up a huge tab after leaving me. The banks hounded me for money I didn't have. One day I attempted to use my credit card, and the storekeeper snatched it from me.

"Bank says I have to," the woman said.

"But that's not fair," I said.

"I'm just doing my job."

I felt humiliated in front of a line of people. The next day, I met with a lawyer about pursuing litigation against Steve for cleaning out our bank accounts and leaving me thousands of dollars in debt. She said I had a good case, but without the $1,000 retainer fee, I could not afford her services.

I continued to see my therapist for weeks of sessions she didn't charge me for. Talking with her helped me keep my head above water, if only barely. If not for therapy, I'm not sure what would've happened. Lauren and Jeff tried reaching out to me, but as usual, I found it almost impossible to reach back. Eventually they left me alone. I felt adrift in California and began thinking about starting over, some place far away.

Knowing I had to do something other than stick my head inside an oven, I applied to and got accepted as a doctoral student at what I will call NP University. (For personal reasons, this school will remain anonymous). So back I went to the Boston area, where I had lived in the mid 1970s as a college freshman. A part-time job and a scholarship awaited me.

My slight familiarity with the Boston area helped me adjust to my new setting, but for the most part I was as lonely as ever. As I became involved in a demanding Ph.D. program in urban planning, I tried to more clearly envision my professional future. My combined experiences of growing up in poverty, spending a year in socially progressive Denmark, and seeing the devastating effects of President Reagan's budget cuts to social programs had inspired in me a strong desire to provide decent, affordable housing for low-income people. My disastrous personal life had sidetracked me from this career path.

Now at age 30, I was as frightened as when I was abruptly snatched from the only foster home I had known. Subsequent years of upheavals from one home to another had deprived me of human attachments. I felt as if I had window-shopped through life, observing other people's personal relationships but failing to develop any myself. I liked animals, but I was even afraid to adopt a pet, fearful a dog or cat would be unexpectedly taken away. What would I do if it died? Continued social isolation, I thought, would prevent the tragedy of further loss. I did not think I could survive any more emotional wounds.

The demand for affordable housing extended to universities. Graduate students and late applicants at the university were not guaranteed dorm rooms, regardless of need. I ended up on a long waiting list.

I had virtually no money. From my student loan, the university deducted my tuition and handed me a check for what little was left. I needed a job, but I was not sure I could handle part-time employment and my studies at the same time. As it was, I was starting my classes off on shaky ground.

Dorm space never materialized. I bounced around in a series of off-campus apartments, some in shabby neighborhoods like the ones I grew up in. When space was unavailable, I slept in homeless shelters.

I lived among the dispossessed—people that were mentally ill, former jail inmates, drug addicts, alcoholics, and sometimes all of those things and more. The few available shelters were over-crowded, in unsafe neighborhoods, and in dilapidated condition. I had not slept on a flimsy cot with a threadbare mattress since my youth. In a fit of depression at the age of 16, I had run away to California. Instead of finding promise in the land of milk and honey, I landed in a residential facility for juvenile offenders. Sleeping in homeless shelters reminded me of those unhappy days.

One chilly night, a haggard-looking black woman waited in line behind me outside the municipal shelter. Beds did not become available until early evening, no matter how bad the weather. The surrounding neighborhood was a collection of shabby houses, littered streets, and garbage-strewn lots. Drug sales were common, as were hookers working their trade.

"What you are doing here?" asked the woman. I noticed her ashy skin, tattered clothes, and frayed shoes.

I generally avoided contact with people at shelters. It was safer that way. But I answered briefly. "I need a place to sleep."

"You got a name, sister?"

"Theresa," I said. "What's yours?"

"Monique Brown," she said, smiling faintly. "All the way from Houston, Texas."

"What brings you to this place?"

"Can't find no work," Monique said. "Without

money, girlfriend, you can't pay no rent. Landlord kicked my ass out. My friends don't got the room, so here I am. Where you from?"

"San Francisco." Burdened with so many bad memories of Buffalo, I told everyone I was from California. I told this lie so often I started to believe it myself.

"Lordy, you're a long way from home. Hey, you talk nice. What you doing here with us hobos?"

"The college didn't have enough dorm space," I said, not sure how much I should reveal about myself.

"For real? Fancy college don't have enough beds for the students? Sounds like the cheap-ass government. I tried to get a place in the projects. Know what they told me? It'd be a seven-year wait. Seven years! What the hell am I supposed to do until then?"

Having worked as a city planner, I was well acquainted with the lack of affordable housing. I was surprised the wait was not longer. "Thank President Reagan for that."

"Screw him and all those tired people in Washington. Let them kiss my black ass," Monique said. She seemed genuinely concerned about me. "Girlfriend, what about you? Got any family who can help?"

"No, I don't."

"Come on, everybody got to have some family. Me and mine don't get along, but I know who they are and where the cheapskates live," Monique said. "So what's your story?"

"I grew up in foster care," I said. "I don't want to get into it."

Monique looked away in embarrassment. "I'm sorry. I'll shut my mouth."

"That's OK."

I never saw her again after that night.

Existence as a homeless person forced upon me realities that most students did not face. My backpack contained what little I owned, including my clothes and personal-hygiene items. I wore my only pair of shoes. I was able to stash some books inside a campus locker, but to be prepared for class I needed to carry most of them with me. I studied in public libraries and ate in soup kitchens. Sometimes I had no money for subway fare, so I hopped the turnstile. I felt shame for not paying my way.

Late one cold, dreary evening I waited in line for the shelter to open. Tiny snowflakes trickled down. I fixed my gaze onto the full moon shimmering in the sky. As I lowered my eyes to check my watch, a scrappy-looking mutt with wiry hair rummaged through a garbage can. Tears swelled in my eyes as I watched the pathetic creature wolf down discarded food scraps. I wanted to help, but what could I do? I was homeless like her. When the dog moved on, a helpless feeling seared my heart. I noticed she had swollen nipples. What had happened to her puppies?

Finally, I confided in a student named Margaret,

who shared a group project with me in one of my courses.

Class had just ended. We shared a cup of hot chocolate in the cafeteria late one afternoon. She noticed me staring at someone's lunch and asked, "Are you hungry?"

I did not want her to think I was sponging off her, but I was famished. She bought me an egg salad sandwich, a cup of vegetable soup, an apple, and a container of juice.

As I ate, she asked, "Do you have a place to live?"

I hoped I did not smell. I tried to keep clean, but I couldn't often find a place to shower. "Not exactly."

"Where have you been staying?"

"In shelters in the city," I said, embarrassed about my plight. I did not want her to think I was a low life.

"Want to live with me? I have an extra room."

"I'll pay you," I said, but I was not sure how I would.

"Get settled first, then worry about money."

Having a decent place to live in a respectable neighborhood was a relief, but it did not affect my basic depression. I wanted to develop a friendship with Margaret, but I shielded my inner self from her. I kept our relationship on a superficial level, talking mostly about my dismay with America's growing involvement in Central America. We shared similar political sentiments, cringing at Ronald Reagan's re-election. For recreation, I wandered around the city. Touring different neighborhoods provided a reprieve from my worsening mental state. Foolishly, I tried to handle my problems on my own.

Lauren hung in there with me. She called one morning as I stared out the window at the ugly gray skies. Another snowstorm was likely to begin at any moment.

"Girl, we're spending the holidays with my folks in New Jersey. I'll buy you a bus ticket, so you have no reason to say no. So will you come?"

"I can't." I had nothing planned.

"Why not?"

"I just can't," I said.

"Stop being you and say yes."

With a lot of prodding, I accepted her invitation and spent three days in New Jersey. I tried to show interest, but I failed. I had lost the ability to even fake feeling alive.

As the spring semester neared an end, preoccupation with death filled my every waking moment. I stopped bathing again. I rarely ate. I stayed awake half the night staring through the darkness. People who talk about suicide often are reaching for help. Those bent on taking their lives usually just do it. As much as I felt like dying, a part of me must have wanted to live because I shared my suicidal thoughts with Margaret. Alarmed and concerned, she urged me to seek help. Reluctantly, I agreed.

I began meeting on and off with an on-campus psychiatrist, a fussy middle-aged man named Dr. Alaverne. I did not like him. He reminded me of neurotic Felix from *The Odd Couple*, but this Felix lacked endearing qualities. As my despondency deepened, so did Margaret's worry. One evening, she heard me on the phone trying to buy an overdose of barbiturates from an illegal mail-order pharmacy.

The next morning, she contacted Dr. Alvarene. He immediately sought a court order to have me committed to a mental hospital.

On June 6, 1985, two campus police officers walked into my last class of the day, handcuffed me, and drove me in a patrol car to a psychiatric hospital. That was the lowest day of my life.

CHAPTER 13

A Shameful Storm

I was admitted to Shady Manor Psychiatric Center, shivering as if it were December. Although strangers had uprooted me many times during my childhood, I had never felt as frightened as I did in the emergency room of a major psychiatric hospital. My legs were so wobbly I could barely stand. Thoughts raced through my mind at a dizzying pace. *What would happen to me? Who could protect me? Who even knew I was there?*

A slender, freckle-faced nurse named Mary said, "Sit down, please." She touched my arm and led me to a nearby chair. I refused to sit.

I twisted around, yanking my body away from her. "I want my lawyer."

I had no lawyer to call, but I was gripped by fear of the unknown. I had seen *One Flew Over the*

Cuckoo's Nest. Mary didn't seem like the vicious Nurse Ratched, but I was terrified by her presence. For all I knew, I was about to be whisked away to undergo a mind-deadening lobotomy.

"We're trying to help you," Mary said.

"Help me by calling a cab and letting me leave," I said, staring into her kindly blue eyes.

Mary remained calm. "Hon, make it easy and answer a few questions, please."

"No," I said. This was jail and I wanted out. Right away.

"How about you nod yes or no to what I ask you?" she said with a tiny smile.

I shrugged my shoulders, but said nothing. Nothing she could do would help me relax.

"Do you know why you're here?"

Still jittery, I finally took a seat. "That doctor had no right sending me here," I said, arms wrapped tightly around my chest. "Call him. He's the one who signed the papers saying I'm crazy."

"Nobody said you're crazy. Dr. Alvarene said you had plans to take your life, and he became worried."

"He could have talked to me instead of sending me here. For God's sakes, this is a *mental hospital*," I said. "I was mortified when my classmates saw me in handcuffs. They probably thought I had done something awful." My usual tightly controlled behavior failed me as I broke down into tears.

"I'm sorry you've had a rough time."

So was I. Soon, I regained a semblance of composure. How could I let strangers see me cry?

"Let me out of here," I begged, my teary eyes studying the room for means of escape. "I want out of here."

"Dear, you're in trouble. Dr. Alvarene thinks we can help you figure out some things."

"Wasn't he thoughtful," I spat.

"There's no need to be sarcastic," Mary said.

Finally, I accepted the nurse's offer of a tissue to wipe away the tears and blow my runny nose. I followed that with a glass of water. I calmed down enough to offer curt replies to the nurse's long list of questions about my medical history, most of which I could not answer. How did I know if hypertension ran in my family, what diseases my parents had, or whether they were ax murderers, for that matter? I had no idea if my biological parents were dead or alive. Fearing someone would jab me with a syringe loaded with a sedative and force me into a straitjacket, I refused to let anyone touch me.

"A doctor will see you in a few minutes," Mary said.

"What for? I'm not sick."

"It's part of the admission process."

"I don't need admitting, I'm leaving," I said. The commotion in the room scared me. A disheveled woman in a skimpy housedress and slippers had just been admitted, screaming about the Republicans next door trying to control her mind.

"You can't leave. The court ordered a ten-day stay," Mary said. "After that, you'll be free to go."

Trying to pretend that I was in control, I stood up. "I'm out of here," I said. "Excuse me, please."

Holding my cold, damp hand, Mary said, "Please don't make this harder on us both. Legally, you have to stay the ten days. That's state law."

"You have no right to do this," I said.

"Yes, we do," she said.

If I bolted, Mary would summon the guards. If I agreed to the admission, would I lose all my rights? I could not bear the idea I needed psychiatric help, but I had run out of options. My tough veneer had cracked.

Despite my fear and resentment, I tried to tone down my hostility. Otherwise I feared they might throw me into isolation or pump me up with powerful sedatives. Mary explained the legal process of voluntary versus involuntary admissions. I listened, realizing I had no choice but to stay. Like a lab animal, I was hopelessly trapped.

A tall, bearded man wearing a snazzy tweed suit, crisp white shirt, and dotted bow tie entered the room and extended his hand. "I'm Dr. Solomon." He spoke with the efficiency of a corporate attorney.

"So," I said, snapping my head so hard it hurt. I refused to accept his handshake or look at his tight face.

"I'm here to continue the admitting process," he said as he reached inside his jacket for a pen. "Let's get going."

"I do not want to be admitted," I said defiantly.

Dr. Solomon sighed.

"Would you like something to calm you down?"

"You can't force that stuff on me." Medication could not undo the hurt caused by a lifetime of depression, loneliness, anger, and fear. I felt like a total failure.

The doctor unbuttoned his jacket and grabbed a manila folder with my name typed on it. I sensed he was in a hurry. "Without your cooperation, I can't help you. Please, let's make this easy, Miss . . ."

"The name is Theresa Cameron, and I don't want your help," I said. "When can I leave?"

He talked out loud as he scribbled notes in my chart. "Patient refuses to cooperate. Admission process will continue tomorrow." He looked at me and said, "When patient is feeling better."

That was the end of my interview with Dr. Solomon. I did not care what else he wrote in my chart. I still fumed about my admission. How could I face my classmates when I returned to school? Presumably many knew I had been taken to a psychiatric hospital. I felt sick wondering what would happen when I returned.

I spent the night inside a tiny, airless room with only a mattress on the floor and a toilet bowl attached to the wall. I was on suicide watch, but I felt like I was in prison. How did they expect me to take my life when all I had on was a sheet-like gown? Hold my breath until I choked? Stripped of everything, except my underwear and socks,

I curled up in a fetal position and cried.

For hours, I tossed and turned, unable to sleep. Without a wall clock, I have no idea how long I stared at the ceiling. Later, I awoke to the sound of Mary's calming voice.

"Wake up, Miss Cameron," she said.

"No," I said, gazing at the mustard-yellow wall.

"It's almost time for breakfast."

"Please leave," I said. "I'm not hungry."

"I'll be back soon, so you can shower," Mary said.

I had not taken a bath in several days, and I felt funky, yet I refused to budge. "I don't need one."

"All our patients shower once a day, including you," Mary said, leaving no room for disagreement.

That morning, I endured several hours of medical tests followed by a round of grilling questioning from Dr. Solomon and Leonard Berco, a social worker, about every aspect of my life, from what I ate for dinner to the regularity of my bowel movements.

Like other professionals I had dealt with over the years, Berco, a young man whose personality was as irritating as sleeping in wet clothing, balked when I said I knew nothing about my biological parents. The uptight man acted as if I withheld important information. "Oh come on, you know nothing?"

"That's right." His snooty attitude made the experience of being in a mental hospital more humiliating than it already was.

"Why didn't you check your records?" he asked.

Since I was never adopted, New York State destroyed my foster care records several years after I left the system. There was nothing to check.

Throughout my childhood, I shouldered the stigma of being a ward of the state. Now I carried the blemish of psychiatric hospitalization, tagged with a diagnosis of "major depression with psychotic features." Considering the twisted route my life had taken, I was surprised I had not broken down before.

What happened over the next days and weeks remains fuzzy. I have kept those memories buried deep inside my psyche. Reliving them now is painful. What follows is my recollection of that time, however imperfect it may be, aided by copies of my hospital records.

A private hospital, Shady Manor was in a leafy suburb of Boston. The surrounding area was solidly upper middle class, overwhelmingly white, and staunchly conservative. The hospital, a well-tended red brick building, was devoid of character. Halls were decorated with the photos of donors, all stuffy-looking white men who had contributed generously to Shady Manor over the years. Patients on public assistance were not generally admitted, unless they had a rare psychiatric disorder like multiple personality. Most patients were white, like the surrounding community. My private insurance through the university covered my admission. Rumors hinted some patients were alcoholics from affluent backgrounds and politically connected families who came to Shady Manor every now and then to dry out. One man, I heard, was a sex offender from a prominent Boston family. Treatment at Shady Manor, instead of a prison sentence, was a deal worked out behind closed doors with the district attorney's office.

I was assigned to a double room on ward B, an L-shaped unit for women. The wealthier patients had private rooms that included meal service, color TVs, bedspreads, drapes, and telephones. My room had no such amenities.

Mary introduced me to my roommate. "I would like you to meet Alice," she said as we walked into a room as plain as a brown paper bag. "Alice, this is Theresa."

I kept my head down and said nothing. I felt humiliated, sharing a room with someone probably as troubled as I.

"Theresa, as soon as you get situated, I'll be back and explain the rest of the routine," Mary said.

I shrugged my shoulders as Mary hurried out of the room.

"When did you come in?" asked Alice, a young woman with short, frizzy brown hair.

"Yesterday," I said.

"I've been here two weeks." Alice spoke matter-of-factly, as if admission to a psychiatric hospital was no big deal. "Want to know why?"

"Yeah, sure," I said. I was surprised I felt somewhat at ease around Alice.

"I slit my wrists," Alice said, holding up freshly sutured scars, "and my parents freaked out from all the blood. My mother was pissed I messed up her new Bill Blass sheets. Screw her. The witch screamed a while, then made a few calls and had me committed."

"Why'd you hurt yourself?"

"It's a long story," she said, glancing at the prominent red wounds on her wrists. "Maybe we'll be in the same group therapy. If not, I'll tell you some other time. What about you?"

"I have a long story, too."

"We'll probably get along just fine then." Alice pulled the sheets over her head. "I'm sleepy from all the pills. See you later."

I watched Alice as she drifted off to sleep. For someone who came so near death, she seemed peaceful, yet her life must have been as hellish as mine, judging from the deep wounds on her wrists. While we talked, the dark skies had unleashed torrents of rain. Sheets of water pelted the windows. As I stared outside at the rain-soaked grounds, I wondered how, when, where, or if I would ever feel better.

The thought of speaking to strangers about my personal life in group therapy made me nauseated. My stomach fluttered, wondering how I would survive a therapist nudging me to open up about my past. I felt a shiver, hoping the group therapist would not be Leonard Berco.

No sooner had I flopped down on my bed and

rolled over when Mary came back. She handed me a chart listing my daily schedule.

"You start individual therapy with Dr. Solomon in half an hour. That's followed by group therapy. After that, it's lunchtime. All meals are served in the dining hall. Unless you're medically cleared, no one is exempted from mealtime."

"Do I have to go through all this?" I said, chewing my lip.

"Yes," she said.

Mary explained that all new patients were treated like buck privates in the Army. Privileges had to be earned. If you complied with the program, you scored points that allowed for smoking time, visits away from the hospital, and snacks between meals. If you missed therapy appointments or fought with other patients or staff, you lost points

Before leaving, Mary handed me a small stack of hospital-issue blouses and slacks. The new outfits, all drab colors, were as plain as a maid's uniform. As I had slid further into depression over the past few months, I had worn the same clothes over and over. I had not changed into a clean outfit for so long Mary had probably tossed my clothing into the trash. If she had not, I might.

Dr. Solomon started our first session with what I thought was an inane question. He asked, "How do you feel?"

"Who wants to know?"

"Miss Cameron, I'm glad you think this is funny," Dr. Solomon said. He was not amused.

Neither was I. Besides feeling fear and confusion, I was lonelier than ever. In addition to 19 years of foster care with multiple placements lasting from several weeks to several years, I endured a troubled marriage, bankruptcy, homelessness, dyslexia, and now admission to a psychiatric center. How was I supposed to feel?

"Please, call me a cab," I said, tapping my foot against the floor.

"Let's talk about why you're here."

"What good will it do?" I said. The tapping intensified. "What about my taxi?"

"It's important you realize how your suicidal behavior has affected you," he said. "And those around you."

"What do you mean, around me? I have no one."

"There's a young lady named Margaret from school who calls. She said she's a friend and is worried about you," Dr. Solomon said. "I'd like to prescribe a course of anti-depressants. Then I'd like to help you gain insights into your depression and how you can get over it."

"I'm not taking anything."

"Medication would help stabilize you."

"What if I refuse?" I asked.

He lifted his eyebrows as if in surprise. "You have the right to say no, but I advise against it."

"Then I say no."

"Theresa, at least give it a try," Dr. Solomon said. "If you don't like it then stop."

"What if it makes me feel worse?"

In the end, I agreed. On one hand, I felt like a dismal failure for my inability to cope with life's pressures. Alternately, I doubted any pill could undo the lingering sadness that filled my soul. But I felt cornered.

Although I resisted my admission at Shady Manor, I felt a glimmer of hope when I entered the group therapy room and found out the therapist was not Leonard Berco. It was Dr. Solomon. And while group therapy was very difficult for me, it did provide me with some insights into my life. I began to realize that for many years, I had been so wrapped up with my suffocating emotions that I had never really understood why I behaved as I did. My abandonment by my mother had set everything in motion. I had never learned that basic, essential attachment—that of a child to its mother. To put the nails in the coffin, I was then denied even a stable foster home. In order to cope, my defense mechanisms had gone into overtime. I became paranoid, suspicious, and defensive, determined that no one would ever get close enough to hurt me. Could I allow Dr. Solomon and his team to drum some sense into my mind? Or would I be pigheaded and continue to clash with everyone who tried to help me?

After the initial involuntary ten-day period elapsed, I was free to leave. As hard as I had fought the idea of entering the hospital, I decided to stay. School was over for the semester. What if Margaret had rented my room to someone else? I was too embarrassed to call her and ask. Making matters worse, I was penniless. At least at Shady Manor I ate three meals a day and had a roof over my head.

One individual therapy session left me sapped. For a few brief moments, I managed to shed the armor locking my emotions inside. I got in touch with some of the rage I felt at my mother for abandoning me as an infant.

"It's OK to be angry," Dr. Solomon said.

Anger would be a mild way of describing how I felt. "How could she do that?" I raged. "I needed her, and she threw me away like garbage. She left me with strangers. A lot of people won't even do that to a dog."

"What does that feel like?" he asked.

I always hated that question. How was it supposed to feel? "It smothered me inside, that's how it feels. She deprived me of my own family. Because of her, I lived in home after home. Some weren't nice. And there was nothing I could do." My throat tightened. "I was just a child, and I was all alone. I'll never forgive her for what she did."

"I didn't say you had to," Dr. Solomon said.

"Good," I snapped, "because I'm not going to."

"What would you say to your mother if you had the chance?"

That question threw me. I stared at the polka-dots on Dr. Solomon's tie. I had played this scenario over in my head time and time again. I had so much to say. Then again, I had nothing to say. It was too painful to think about. It was better to want nothing to do with her, just as she had wanted nothing to do with me. I ended the session early and retreated to my room.

I was relieved to see that Alice was out. So many painful thoughts pressed on my mind. I curled up in bed and drew the covers over my head.

The session with Dr. Solomon made me think of an old Negro spiritual called "Were You There?" In my mind that night, I mentally addressed that question to the woman who had given me birth. "Were you there when they took me away?" I asked her. "Were you there when they moved me from home to home? Were you there when they told me I was retarded? Were you there when they molested me? Were you there when I sobbed at night for you? Were you there when I tried to kill myself?" I cried myself to sleep singing the words to "Were You There?"

My stay at Shady Manor grew quite stormy. I was deeply conflicted about being there. Clearly part of me wanted the help the staff was trying to give me. But a lifetime of keeping people at arm's length had made it almost impossible to accept that help. In my confusion, stubbornness, and fear, I kept handing in "three-day notices." The notice was a legal form that announced that a patient would be leaving in three days. Filling out a three-day notice gave me a warped sense of empowerment. As a foster child, I had no choice with whom I lived or for how long I stayed. At the age of 31, no one was about to push me around.

On my eleventh voluntary day at Shady Manor, I filled out yet another three-day notice and handed it to Dr. Solomon at the beginning of our therapy session. Stroking his neatly clipped beard, he looked at me and said, "And what's the purpose of this?"

"So you can wish me good luck," I said.

"How come you want to leave?"

"I don't belong here."

"I think you do," Dr. Solomon said.

"You can't keep me against my will," I said.

"No, not anymore. You're free to leave."

By the time group therapy rolled around, I changed my mind. I sat through the session, avoiding Dr. Solomon's occasional glances. I barely participated, even though I had a lot on my mind. I was as obstinate as they came. Probably irritating, too.

Another twisted way I tried to exert control over my life was by lying about taking my medication. I acted as if I took the pills, but I held them underneath my tongue, then spit them out when no one was looking.

During our therapy session one day, Dr. Solomon said, "Are you taking your medication?"

I squirmed in my seat. "Why?"

"Your blood levels of Desipramine should be higher," he said. "Makes me wonder."

"Are you accusing me of something?" I said, heart racing.

"Let me ask you again, are taking your medication as prescribed?"

"Yes," I said, knowing I was lying.

"I don't believe you are. Your blood levels should be much higher than they are. If you're not taking the medication, you're hurting yourself, not me."

Much later, I realized how destructive my actions had been. Overwhelmed with pain, I manipulated situations to avoid looking at emotional wounds that never healed. I engaged in game playing with the hospital staff, although at the time I had little or no insight into my foolish behavior.

During a therapy session not much later, Dr. Solomon brought up my repeated use of the three-day notice.

"Why do you submit, then retract a three-day notice?"

I felt on the spot. I had no logical explanation for my actions. "What do you mean?"

"You know what I'm talking about," Dr. Solomon said. He was as stiff as always. "Since your admission, you've already handed in four three-day notices. You've changed your mind every time."

"So?" I felt the muscles in my stomach tighten.

"Is this your way of getting attention from the staff, from me?"

Beads of sweat trickled down my face as I threw up my guard. "You're wrong."

"Then tell me what's behind this."

I walked out of his office, rejecting group activities for the rest of the day. I stayed in my room, shutting off questions from Alice as well.

*   *   *

On June 25, 1985, I retracted a three-day notice. Two days later, I submitted yet another one. The staff labeled me as a challenging, conniving patient. Dr. Solomon said if I submitted another notice, he would discharge me. On July 17, 1985, I handed in another. I was told to leave.

I took little from my hospitalization except a bag of frumpy clothes and two subway tokens. I still lacked insight into my behavior, and I was still choked by depression. Would I always live on the emotional fringes of life?

CHAPTER 14

Rebuilding Myself

As I walked away from Shady Manor, I felt as lost as I did on my last day of foster care. I was totally numb. If someone had asked me a simple question, I could not have answered. What was I expected to do? The child-welfare system took care of me for years. I did not have to make decisions for myself. Catholic Charities made them for me. For the past five weeks, the doctors and therapists at Shady Manor ruled my life. What would I do now that I was on my own? Could I cope?

I stood on an empty corner waiting for a bus to nowhere. The weather was hot and humid. Drenched in sweat, I reached inside my pocket and fiddled with the tokens I'd been given before leaving Shady Manor. That plus $25, a soup kitchen voucher, and directions to the nearest women's shelter was all I had.

Like a runaway, I wandered around the city all day, hopping on and off different buses and trains. I had absolutely no appetite. I gave my voucher to a homeless woman I met on the Red Line subway. As nightfall approached, I reluctantly found my way to the women's shelter. I was too afraid to sleep on a park bench alone.

Boston's only women's shelter was as dingy and dreary as something out of a Charles Dickens novel. Inside one large cavernous room, row after row of Army-style cots were lined up. Because it was summer, the shelter was not packed as it was in winter. I hurried to grab a cot near a wall. The thought of sleeping in the midst of so many strangers sent chills up my spine. I lay awake, gazing at the ceiling. Some women were ex-cons looking for trouble, but most were ragged-looking mental patients. When medications that could more or less control delusions were introduced in the late 1960s, publicly funded mental hospitals discharged thousands of patients. There was only one problem. Government funded follow-up programs to care for these people never materialized. Single room occupancy hotels (SROs), once a stable source of housing for the mentally ill, had all but disappeared. SRO owners converted the hotels to luxury housing. This was tough luck for the mentally ill and other dispossessed souls, most of whom became homeless. Needless to say, I slept very little that night.

The next morning I woke up feeling grungy, tired, and hungry. I craved a hot bath, clean underwear, and a bowl of Cheerios with raisins and cold milk. For safety, I hid my money, including coins, inside my shoe. Homeless shelters are filled with needy people who sometimes rip off other residents.

By 6 a.m. everyone had to be awake and dressed for breakfast, which that day consisted of stale powdered donuts and coffee so weak I could see through it. There were filthy toilets, sinks clogged with hair and cigarette ashes, and no shower facilities. After breakfast, the shelter cleared out until nightfall. No one was allowed inside during the day, even during severe weather. At least it was not raining.

I skipped the food and left right away. At the nearest pay phone, I fished a few coins out of my shoe and made a call to Margaret. *Please, please have room available*, I thought.

My hands shook as I fed a dime into the phone. By the 10th ring, I was about to hang up when she answered. "Hi, it's Theresa," I said. "Remember me?"

Panting slightly, she said, "I just walked through the door when I heard the phone ringing. Of course I remember. How are you?"

"I'm not in the hospital anymore."

"Where are you?" Margaret asked.

"Downtown. I just left the shelter."

"Stay with me for a while," she said.

"Are you sure?" I asked.

"I'll have something ready to eat when you get here."

I stayed with Margaret for a few weeks until I regained my footing. After three or four job interviews, which I attended in borrowed clothes, I found work as a city planner with a private agency in Boston. The job was reasonably interesting, the salary kept me off the streets, and I liked being part of the workforce again. I ditched my wardrobe of second-hand clothes and bargain-basement discards. I even started a small savings account. I found a place to stay, sharing an apartment with a graduate student named Max. Max was a white woman, but I felt more comfortable with her than I did with many of the black students in the area, most of whom were from middle-class backgrounds. Max had grown up in poverty in rural Kentucky. She was a poet and a socialist who lived simply, as much by her own preference as by necessity. I didn't feel like quite such an oddball around Max.

The Boston of the 1980s was a different place from the late 1970s, when I last lived there. At that time, forced busing to integrate the public-school system spawned ugly protests. Race relations were so tense they came close to exploding. The South Boston and Charlestown neighborhoods had been totally off limits to blacks. Jim Crow, once thought to be dead, was alive and well in these white strongholds.

By the mid-1980s busing was no longer a

heated issue. Public housing in South Boston and Charlestown integrated under court orders that threatened heavy fines for non-compliance. Despite steady social change, crushing poverty lingered in the black ghettos of Dorchester, Mattapan, and Roxbury. For years, the housing and infrastructure needs of these areas were virtually ignored by city government. Some homes resembled the rickety shacks so common throughout the South. Streets were often gutted and full of potholes.

Memories of the vast social welfare network that crisscrossed the lives of Danish citizens remained with me. I often wondered why the U.S. never tried to install such a system. Access to housing, healthcare, education, etc. was available to all Europeans. A much different arrangement prevailed in the U.S. I hoped my work as a planner could, at least in a small way, alter the lives of poor blacks by opening up affordable housing to people who lived in squalor.

As only one of two blacks working at this housing agency, I was immediately drawn to the other, Judy Clark, also a planner. Almost overnight, we became friends. At lunchtime, we wandered around the narrow streets of downtown Boston. It was densely packed with office buildings and hotels, with several subway lines converging on the area. Nearby were important landmarks such as Quincy Market, City Hall, and Haymarket Square, not to mention other significant sites, such as department stores Jordan Marsh and Filene's.

Judy always wore stylish clothes. At least twice a week, she prodded me to join her for a shopping foray into Filene's Basement, one of her favorite haunts. Filene's Basement, as I had learned as a college freshman, offered an array of clothing from bargain basement styles to designer imports at reduced costs. Grudgingly, I went along. I never liked shopping in crowded stores, but I was amused by Judy's ability to sniff out a good deal, even among throngs of avid shoppers. Most times, we returned from lunch with Judy dragging a shopping bag loaded with new clothes. As I soon learned, Judy was fickle. Why was I not surprised the next day when she asked me to join her at Filene's to return what she bought the day before?

As Judy's wardrobe expanded, so did mine. The garments she did not like, she often gave to me. Sometimes the hand-me-downs were almost brand-new. I started feeling better about myself again.

On a sunny but blustery Saturday afternoon, Judy and I meandered around Quincy Market to search for additional bargains. Cold weather failed to deter Judy from shopping. She had her limits, though. Judy ventured into the rain only if absolutely necessary.

The subject of family ties came up that casual afternoon. Judy knew my basic story. As a rule, I shied away from questions regarding my past, but I liked Judy so I did not cut her off.

"Aren't you curious about your roots?"

"No," I said, trusting my terse reply would steer the conversation in another direction, any direction. It did not.

"Get real, girl, you don't want to know about your family? What your cousins are like? If sickle cell runs in your genes?" Sickle cell anemia is a blood disorder that primarily affects people of African descent.

"I'd know by now if I had the disease," I said.

We stopped in a coffee shop to warm up. After removing our coats and hats, we took seats inside a cozy booth. Stirring her mug of hot chocolate, Judy asked, "Aren't you curious to see whom you look like?"

"No," I said. My eyes fixated on the whipped cream slowly melting inside my mug.

"You may have siblings."

Part of me did care. I was frightened to know the truth, so I never bothered to dip into my past. What if my mother turned out to be a low life, a prostitute, or a crack addict, or my father was in jail for murder? My fear of further rejection played an important role, too. Perhaps my birth mother and/or father would view my efforts to find them as intrusive. I had always believed I was abandoned for a reason. Was it wise to stir up old history? I decided to let sleeping dogs lie. Besides, without foster care records, my search would likely have been fruitless.

Cramps tightened my stomach, so I said, "Let's talk about something else. Are you still seeing Rodney?"

"You're impossible, but I hear you. And yes, I am still seeing Rodney. At least for now."

The conversation shifted to Judy's love life and her up and down relationship with Rodney. One day, she wanted to marry him, then the next day she would be ready to call it quits. At least she had a love life, which is more than I could say about myself. Except for my friendship with Judy and a casual relationship with Max, I remained as reclusive as ever. With the social skills of a misfit, I lived in a carefully guarded world. I was the mistress of my universe, yet sometimes my universe nearly stifled me to death.

My job was reasonably fulfilling. Our agency worked to secure funding to renovate dilapidated housing, then resell it at affordable rates to poor people, most of whom were black. Securing money from the government for affordable housing was harder than convincing banks to do business in the ghetto. The more I learned about the business of affordable housing, the angrier I became. Demand far outstripped supply. Landlords abandoned properties in poor neighborhoods because they could not pay the taxes or could no longer squeeze out a profit. Virtually no new public housing was built. As a result, homelessness shot up, and the city housed people in rundown welfare motels or in overcrowded shelters. No one seemed to care, either, because most of those affected were poor and minority. Our agency was trying to fight a forest fire with a garden hose. We could not help everyone.

*　　*　　*

For many reasons, I wanted a doctorate. The job market for blacks remained uncertain, even for educated women like Judy and me. I hoped an advanced degree would shield me from the soup kitchens, although it was no guarantee. Holding a doctorate would also be the ultimate achievement for an unwanted kid from the ghetto. A doctorate would prove to myself that I might be bruised, but I was not broken.

I mulled over the idea for a while before finally discussing it with Judy. Over dinner at a Chinese restaurant, she said, "Where do you plan to apply?"

"I haven't decided yet."

"What about Harvard?" Judy asked as she devoured a plate loaded with egg foo yung, dumplings, beef with oyster sauce, and white rice. As thin as a string bean, Judy had the voracious appetite of a construction worker. "That's across the bridge. We can still see each other." She referred to the popular Massachusetts Avenue Bridge linking Boston and Cambridge.

"Harvard! You must be kidding," I said almost gagging on a bite of fried rice.

"I'm serious," Judy said. Our eyes locked. "Why not?" Harvard was only the country's most prestigious university. "They won't take me."

"How do you know unless you apply?"

Over the next few weeks, I compiled a list of schools with urban planning programs that interested me, and called for catalogs. Almost daily, an information packet arrived with pictures of smiling students on picturesque campuses. Colleges and universities were still predominantly white. Affirmative action programs had opened the doors for many black students, but far too many lingered in dead-end jobs with only a marginal high school education. Higher education, even in public universities, came with a price. Due to a fluctuating economy, rising unemployment, and reduced public aid for tuition, a lot of students needed financial aid. A doctorate seemed out of reach for a financially strapped student like me.

Every time I picked up the phone to call Harvard for an application, I froze. My palms became so sweaty I had trouble grasping the receiver. After the eighth try, I finally stayed on the line, but I wasn't sure I could speak.

"May I help you?" a friendly voice asked. This was 1988, so the glut of automated answering systems had not yet arrived. Real people answered phones then. If I had had to push button after button, only to leave my name at the sound of a tone, I probably would have given up. Modern technology often frustrated me. It still does.

I stammered for a second and then said, "I'd like an application, please. For the doctoral program. Thank you for your help."

"Wait, who are you? Where do I send it?"

"Oh, that's right." Once I told her my name and address, I said, "I need an application for financial aid."

"That's part of the package I'm sending."

"Thanks again," I said.

"Good luck," she said.

She hadn't laughed at me, or hung up on me, or demanded to know why I thought I deserved to go to Harvard. Maybe Judy was right, I thought. If I did not apply, I would never know if I would be accepted.

In the spring of 1989, the Harvard University Graduate School of Design accepted my application. Initially, I was stunned. I could hardly believe that I had arrived in the big leagues. That acceptance call was one of the proudest moments of my life. The nuns who had said I was stupid, even retarded, would have to reconsider their opinion.

I called Judy to tell her the news. My roommate Max congratulated me, but her socialist views meant she despised the Ivy League. She said Harvard was run by a small group of conservative and wealthy white men. Maybe so, but I valued my acceptance. Foster care would never define me again.

Judy treated me to Indian food at a family-owned restaurant in Central Square in Cambridge. "So, Miss Thing, you made it. I'm proud of you."

I managed a shy grin. "Thanks. You were the one who convinced me I could make it there."

"Who will I go shopping with at lunch time?" Judy lamented. "I'll have to wait in the return line all alone."

"I think you'll manage. We can still see each other, you know," I said. "Maybe even go shopping to Filene's."

"I'd like that," Judy said.

On my last day at the job, Judy and my coworkers threw a small going-away party. They ordered a three-layer chocolate cake with gooey icing and bought me a leather briefcase. All 20 employees signed a farewell card. I was surprised at how many people said they would miss me. I walked out the door that day hoping I had made the right decision. Was I crazy to think I could handle the rigorous demands at Harvard?

CHAPTER 15

The World According to Harvard

The financial-aid package covered tuition but not meals, books, housing, or fees. Since my checking account was nearly empty, I had to work part-time. Harvard had promised me a job that did not involve wiping cafeteria tables or scouring toilets. I hoped they meant it.

I also needed another place to live. Living with a minimally employed poet did not offer the stability I needed to work through graduate school. I told Max I was moving. She sobbed, wrote a poem, and wished me good luck.

Dormitory space for graduate students was limited, so I looked on the open market. Just as well. I was not thrilled at the idea of living in a dorm at the age of thirty-five. The rental rates in mostly affluent Cambridge were so high that I doubted I could afford my own place. I studied the newspapers for apartment shares. I considered asking Judy to share a place, but her on-again, off-again relationship with Rodney posed a problem. What if we rented an apartment and she got married? Then I would be stuck with rent I had no way of paying. As a full-time doctoral student, I would hardly have time to look for another roommate.

On a Sunday afternoon in late May, I checked out six apartments, none of which seemed right. One woman lived in a fabulous neighborhood, but she smoked. Another couple had a spacious extra room on a leafy block in a ritzy neighborhood, but since neither worked, I suspected they were up to no good, maybe selling drugs. Scrap that one, too. I flat out refused to live with someone who kept tarantulas as pets. By late afternoon, I was tired, hungry, and concerned I might not find a place to live. In a few days, I had to start my part-time job at Harvard. There was one ad left.

"Do you like dogs?" a woman asked over the din of barking.

"Yes," I said, straining to hear.

"Then come over."

"Don't you want to know my name? Or that I'm black?"

"Can you pay the rent?"

"I sure can," I said.

"When are you coming?"

We sealed a deal. In exchange for half the rent and utilities along with occasional dog walking, I would share a two-bedroom apartment in a three-story building with Kathy and her two mutts in an area called East Cambridge.

Lower-income East Cambridge was home to predominantly working-class people of Portuguese background. Portuguese-language signs hung in many store windows. There was even a public housing project, a rarity closer to Harvard. No one in the largely white neighborhood seemed to notice my skin color as I walked down the side streets towards the bus stop on Massachusetts Avenue. All my things were still with Max and I had to pack. I told my new roommate, Kathy, I would be back in the morning. As had always been the case, everything I owned fit into shopping bags.

Harvard University was like a city unto itself. The campus cut a huge swath from Massachusetts Avenue in central Cambridge and sprawled eastward along the very polluted Charles River. City streets crisscrossed the campus. Traffic was steady most of the day, and at rush hour there were often monster jams. Unlike downtown Boston where impatient drivers leaned on car horns, drivers stuck in Cambridge traffic displayed political correctness by not honking. Sometimes it all seemed unreal. In the two years I lived there, I never saw a cab driver stick his head out the window and yell, "Hey Mack, move that piece of shit out of here," followed by a blare of the horn and an obscene gesture.

Red brick buildings on campus were two to three-story structures, all in superb condition. Any broken windows or loose hinges, common sights in the ghetto neighborhoods I grew up in, were quickly tended to by the grounds crew. Lawns were clipped regularly and virtually free from trash Huge oak trees, neatly pruned bushes, and squirrels munching on nuts added to the bucolic New England setting.

Most of the professors and students were white. Blacks were generally restricted to menial jobs such as maintenance, food service, or clerical work. A few famous blacks taught at Harvard, such as former law school Professor Derrick Bell, but on the whole there were a handful of tenured black faculty or students.

The Harvard elite lived in tony neighborhoods surrounding campus, where homes fetched exorbitant prices. Almost all the posh, brick apartment buildings and single-family homes looked like they should be featured in an architectural magazine. Highly paid professors and administrators shopped in upscale stores that lined Massachusetts Avenue and dined in restaurants where the cost of one dinner could feed me for a week.

Once when I was eating lunch alone in a university cafeteria, another student asked me, "Oh Miss, please wipe this table? It's dirty."

Some people I know would have told her to wipe their ass. But blowing up was out of character for me, even when my blood boiled. "I'm a student. I don't work here."

Her red face showed she was embarrassed. Before leaving I said, "There ARE black students at Harvard."

Superior attitudes, common throughout Harvard, annoyed me. Sure, some students were as low-key as I, but many reveled in being Harvard students and often draped themselves in college attire from head to toe.

A snobbish student in my program, sporting her new Harvard T-shirt, found me outside of class. Strutting down the corridor like a fashion model, she said, "Doesn't this look nice on me?"

I pretended not to hear her, but she persisted and caught up with me.

"Theresa, what do you think?" The woman smiled as she threw herself in front of me.

"About what?" I said.

She seemed genuinely hurt. "My new shirt?"

"My mind was on something else. Your shirt looks fine. I'm late for lunch. Catch you later."

I left without turning around. Part of me felt sorry for her, as annoying as she was. As I walked across the street, I heard her say, "Excuse me, but doesn't this shirt look terrific on me?"

Once I settled into my new living arrangement, I started work at one of Harvard's many think tanks. There I had to read endless government and other reports about housing, picking out relevant facts and figures that Harvard used for its own reports. Because the reading material was mostly statistical in nature, I became bored. It was a miracle I passed statistics in college. Scanning the material also saddened me. The push to provide affordable housing was diminishing, while homelessness, especially among families with dependent children, had increased. Government aid involved increasing overnight shelters, not subsidized housing.

To view homelessness firsthand, I only needed to venture out to Harvard Square at lunchtime. Much to the annoyance of shop owners and local residents, the dispossessed clung to wobbly shopping wagons loaded with their meager belongings as they panhandled by the train station. Most of the homeless were black men and women. I had a hard time looking into the vacant eyes of these lost souls begging on the streets. I was in Cambridge, yet sometimes I felt like I was in a third world country. Instead, I had just been accepted into what was probably the world's most prestigious and costly university. The mere mention of attending Harvard elevated a student to a higher level. Parents shelled out tens of thousands of dollars for their children to attend the school. Students who received rejection notices from Harvard's admission office were emotionally crushed. There I was, staring at ashy-skinned men and women wearing urine-soaked pants as they rifled through dumpsters outside fancy restaurants, searching for scraps of food. As much as I hated to think about it, I could have easily been one of those people thrusting an empty coffee cup into a stranger's face while pleading for a handout. For whatever reasons, some of which I still cannot explain, I escaped the hardships of street life. I hoped my Harvard education would keep it that way.

*   *   *

Living with Kathy's dogs, Holly and Henry, was fun. I had never lived with pets. Holly, a floppy-eared three-year-old cross among collie, beagle, and whatever, was a happy- go-lucky dog who showered affection upon me. She loved to be loved. If Kathy was busy, Holly played lapdog with me, except she was bigger than my lap.

Henry, a few years older, was more reserved. Kathy said he had been abused as a puppy. She rescued him from a neighbor who routinely beat him with a broom. She never did say, but I suspected that Kathy and one of her animal-loving friends stole Henry. I am glad they did. Quiet and dignified, Henry was also loyal and loving. I enjoyed taking the two dogs out for walks. Strolling through the neighborhood relaxed me and allowed me to meet our neighbors. Only one or two miscreants uttered racially derogatory remarks. The other neighbors were cautiously polite, but otherwise left me alone.

Our living situation was comfortable enough. The apartment was cramped, but we managed. Kathy was a hospital social worker on the evening shift. We did not see much of each other during the week. Now and then, we went to dinner and a movie.

Kathy had a peculiar habit that puzzled me for a few weeks, until I felt I knew her well enough to ask about it. Although we lived about two miles from Harvard's main campus, Kathy routinely drove her dogs there and let them romp around the university's grounds. In our neighborhood, she always picked up after them when they eliminated. At Harvard, she never did.

After she returned from one of her trips to the campus, I asked, "Why do you drive all the way over there when there's a park two blocks away?"

"Because I like when they shit on Harvard. It's my way of getting back."

"Did something happen with you and Harvard?" I wondered if she had applied for admission or a job and had been rejected.

"No, I just hate the way they use city services and don't pay their fair share of taxes. Screw them and the pompous snobs who go there. I know it probably sounds stupid, but it's a habit I got into and it makes me feel better."

I kept in touch with my good friend Judy from the city planning office. I once broke down and joined her for a shopping jaunt in Filene's Basement, her favorite hangout. How could I say no? Judy swore she was through with Rodney. She asked me to share an apartment, an offer I declined. Somehow, I always thought they would get back together.

Researching, writing, and defending a thesis were the key aspects of the doctoral program I enrolled in. Almost immediately, I had to come up with a topic. But what would I choose?

By 1989, the plight of infants born with AIDS

was splashed across the headlines. Most of these babies were black or Hispanic and were born to crack-addicted mothers, many of whom abandoned them at birth. I felt a special bond with these rejected babies. They were often referred to as "boarder babies" because they were abandoned in the municipal hospitals where they were born. Hospitals viewed them as temporary boarders.

In the 1980s, ignorance about AIDS was widespread. People still believed it could be spread through a handshake or sitting on a toilet seat. Not surprisingly, child welfare authorities had significant trouble placing foster babies. Fear and ignorance stranded many infants at hospitals for up to a year, sometimes longer. So that babies would not be deprived of human contact in those crucial early stages, hospitals responded by recruiting hundreds of empathetic volunteers, who did nothing except cuddle and nurture those helpless infants.

My interest in the situation led me to focus on housing for children with AIDS as my thesis topic. A few misinformed professors on my thesis committee did not see how boarder babies related to the field of design. It was my job to explain.

In the midst of a private meeting, one of my advisors, Professor Ben Worth, said, "Consider another topic. I'm not sure these babies are an appropriate choice for a degree in design."

"I disagree," I said.

"It's easy to be emotional over them, but please stick to design. Let the social workers worry about the babies."

Selling him on my concept needed a fight. "May I explain?"

"OK, go ahead, but I don't think it's a good idea."

I went to work, outlining the problem. Then I explained the difficulty involved with placement. So far so good. He paid attention, but the scowl on his face told me he remained uncertain. "How and when does design come in?"

"Placing these children into foster homes has been nearly impossible. They can't grow up in hospital nurseries. I've read of a few group homes that have opened just for boarder babies."

He stroked his chin as he said, "Go on."

"Because they have an infectious disease, these infants have special needs. Caring for them isn't like caring for the average baby. And that is where design comes in."

"How will you research this?"

"By looking at existing group homes for children with AIDS and other facilities that care for chronically ill children, like the Ronald McDonald Houses."

"It's a stretch, a long stretch, but I'm willing to give it a shot. Go ahead with your idea. Meet me tomorrow at this time and we'll hammer out the details."

I left his office feeling elated. After eating lunch outside on one of the many benches lining Harvard's campus, I realized I had a lot of work to do.

As the first black student accepted at the School of Design, I felt extra pressure to achieve.

If I botched the program, I worried black students who came after me might be judged by my failure. I was constantly afraid of faltering. Not only was I representing Theresa Cameron, but I was also there on behalf of my race. I felt I had to uphold higher standards than other students. No one, however, treated me any differently. I became like one of the guys (most of my fellow students were men). Still, I had my doubts. Would my slip-ups be judged more critically than those of my white peers? Yes, I thought they would be. Was that fair? No, of course not. But in my view our society, for all its positive changes, was still mired in racism that desperately needed correction.

My schedule was packed. Attendance in my design classes was mandatory, but working on the thesis consumed huge chunks of time. I needed to travel, because only a handful of long-term care facilities for children with AIDS existed, and none were in the Boston area. I planned visits to a group home in New Jersey and a hospital ward in New York City that also served as a temporary residence. In addition, I scheduled a visit to a Ronald McDonald House in Boston. Located near many major hospitals, Ronald McDonald Houses were funded by the McDonald's corporation to serve as temporary homes for seriously ill children who needed overnight medical treatment, as well as their parents. Sometimes children from rural areas needed care available only in cities. Parents who were strapped for money could hardly afford hotel bills on top of medical care, so McDonald's helped fill the gap by funding Ronald McDonald Houses.

On each visit, I studied the layout of the building, researched local building codes, and asked employees for design recommendations. I also researched the problem of NIMBYism. NIMBY is an acronym for "Not In My Back Yard." It describes the attitude of citizens who might support the principle of group homes or long-term care facilities, but who oppose such facilities going up anywhere near their own homes. My research showed just how difficult it would be to find friendly neighbors for children with AIDS.

Once I conducted on-site visits, I had to sort through reams of data and organize them in a workable form. Since I couldn't afford a home computer, I spent the greater part of two years working on my thesis in one of Harvard's many computer labs. Quite often, I worked on weekends and nights at school. In other words, my social life was almost non-existent. What else was new? At the same time, I was surrounded by a small group of classmates who were supportive as well as helpful. They were not competitive at all, as I feared they might be.

The School of Design only had about 23 students, so we had ample opportunity to get to know one another in the design studio or in the classroom. I was particularly drawn to another student named Jay and his wife Donna, who provided me with what little social life I did have. Jay, who had already earned a master's degree in computer science from another Ivy League college, was enrolled for a master's degree in computer-aided design. Donna held a job outside the university. She was around so frequently, it seemed like she was part of the design program. The three of us became friends right away. Somehow with those two, I didn't feel the need to act my usual role of the recluse.

Because I commuted to school via bus or bike, Jay often gave me a lift. I particularly appreciated his generosity during the winter months when pedaling across Massachusetts Avenue against blustery winds turned into a formidable challenge. Donna sometimes treated me to lunch. Jay's mother and sister were both physicians, and Donna's father was very successful in business, yet they never bragged about their privileged backgrounds. The three of us often ate dinner in one of the many restaurants in and around Central and Harvard Square. Now and then, we went to the movies or an art museum in Boston.

In the springtime, we watched the annual regatta where crew teams from colleges across the Northeast competed. Hundreds of spectators, including raucous fans from the many schools represented, lined the public parks along both sides of the narrow river to cheer on their teams. As I had so many years before when I was a college fresh-man, I enjoyed watching groups of energetic students power the slender, sleek boats that seemed to glide effortlessly up and down the Charles River.

Beyond simply offering their friendship, Jeff

and Donna provided invaluable editing help by reading and re-reading my dissertation. Perhaps they got bored revising the same material over and over. Sometimes even I did, but they never said so. I doubt I could have finished my degree without their steady assistance. To this day, I treasure their friendship as I do few from the Harvard years. Distance has separated us for many years, but we talk on the phone regularly. When possible, we see each other in person.

The high cost of living in the Boston area almost did me in. Kathy and I lived in a three-story apartment building that lacked any shred of character in a working-class neighborhood, but the rent was high. My first job at Harvard ended. My savings from it plus my financial-aid package saw me through my first year. To make ends meet in the summer of 1990, I found a job babysitting a neighbor's child. Quite often, Kathy shared her groceries with me. Several times, I applied for and received financial assistance from a private charity. Now and then, my friend Judy treated me to dinner. My old friend Max the poet still believed she would become a best-selling author. Maybe someday she would.

I spent Christmas time with Kathy and her dogs. Kathy doted on them. At Christmas, she lavished them with stockings that held squeaky toys, chew bones, and tasty snacks. She even took them to a large shelter and paid to have them photographed with Santa Claus. She bought them new sweaters, since winters in Boston were some-times brutally cold. The dogs protested, however, when she tried putting on rubber booties to protect their paws. I laughed until I nearly cried as Kathy strapped a bootie on each paw, only to see the dogs frantically kick their legs and shake off the doggie boots. After numerous tries, she finally gave up.

After endless hours at the computer lab and the library, I finally produced a rough draft of my thesis. I then went to work fine-tuning it with the help of Professor Worth. Despite his initial reservations about my topic, he remained a steady and consistent advisor. His guidance was influential in my achievements at Harvard. As the second year drew to a close, it became clear I had completed the requirements for a doctorate. On a glorious spring day when sunshine streaked across clear blue skies, I successfully defended my thesis. I was in heaven, although I refused to share my elation with my classmates, acting cordial as if it was just another ordinary day. I did spring for the cost of a cap and gown and walked down the aisle to receive my diploma. This unwanted black baby who spent 19 years as a ward of New York State had earned a doctorate in design from Harvard University. I was *Dr.* Theresa Cameron

CHAPTER 16

Today

Since that memorable day when I received my degree from Harvard, I've held teaching posts at several colleges before arriving at my current position at Arizona State University. I've continued to concentrate my research and teaching on housing, often remembering the rat- and roach-infested foster homes I grew up in, as well as the homeless shelters and abandoned cars I sometimes inhabited as a graduate student. I was impressed with the European system of public housing when I attended college in Denmark in the 1970s. I wonder to this day why the U.S., the richest country in the world, cannot manage to construct such a system. Instead, since the 1980s, our federal government has eroded support for subsidized housing until almost none exists. Disadvantaged people—

including foster children like me, leaving the system with a high school diploma and no marketable skills—simply cannot earn enough money to afford a market rate apartment. To stay afloat, they need special help. Otherwise, they may be tempted by gangs, drugs, or a life of crime. I am still amazed that didn't happen to me.

On a personal level, not a great deal has changed for me. Over the years I dated once in a while, but never married again. It's not simply that I've gone through a divorce that has made me avoid romance. Relationships don't always work out—that's a risk we all take. But when my ex-husband emptied our bank account and stranded me with thousands of dollars of debt, I was shattered. After our crushing breakup, I was never the same. I don't pretend that I was the ideal partner, but I didn't deserve to be betrayed like that. It took me years to regain my confidence and dignity.

I've been more successful putting my energies into volunteer organizations devoted to foster children. For a while I served as board president of a group that raised money to buy special items that foster care doesn't pay for, like toys, computers, books, and enrollment in sports programs. I worked with terrific people and took pride and pleasure in my work. The children were so appreciative of our efforts. I reluctantly left that organization when it interfered with my teaching and research demands at ASU.

*   *   *

Later, I volunteered as a pet therapist with an organization called "Gabriel's Angels." Gabriel's Angels uses pets to try to break the cycle of violence in abused and at-risk children. The children I visited were homeless. Initially, I felt discouraged because the children needed so much more than I thought I had to offer. I wondered what good I could do there with Luke, one of the stray dogs that my housemate had adopted. I didn't realize that teaching children about compassion, respect, and kindness was just as important as providing for their material needs. I temporarily dropped out of the program, but I hope to resume pet therapy soon. In the meantime, every holiday season, I organize a toy drive for the organization.

I own my own home in Tempe. For the last several years, I have shared it with a friend who was disabled in a serious car accident. Due to the lack of subsidized housing for disabled people, she cannot afford to live alone. So I invited her and her two dogs to share my home. Debra is involved with animal rescue, and at times we've had as many as seven dogs living with us. Although I rarely allow myself to become close to people or pets, I became unusually attached to a dachshund named Oscar. He lived with us for about a year. Crying doesn't come easily to me, but I shed tears when Oscar died. I still miss that dog, even though he was crabby and irritable most of the time. He came from a home where he was kept outside all the time and rarely socialized. I felt like I understood Oscar.

Foster care robbed me of emotions. I've been afraid to love someone, fearing that at any moment they could be ripped from me. I was thrown into a position of uncertainty where I could never put down roots. I didn't know who I belonged to. I was never told the truth behind my abandonment. Many of my foster siblings at least knew their families and the system often made plans for their return. I had no family to be returned to. On top of all that, I had learning difficulties that were never addressed. Nuns who were supposed to be God's messengers on Earth called me stupid. Light-skinned blacks deepened my pain when they called me names like "darkie" and "brownie." Maybe none of this would've happened if my birth mother had signed the documents to free me for adoption. Then again, maybe she was never told that adoption was even an option. She was only sixteen. Maybe she was a victim of rape. I'll never know what really happened.

I've spent much of my life chronically depressed, deeply private, and largely aloof because of circumstances that were beyond my control. I've spent hours in therapy trying to cope with my past. Moving forward is a struggle, and frankly I have sometimes wondered if it's worth the effort. But then I look at how others fight back and I feel inspired. I take comfort from the good friends who have hung in there with me, as well as my cherished pets.

* * *

I realize now that no matter how hard I try to overcome my past, it will always be with me. I hid behind the shame of it for many years , but it was shame over things that were never my fault. I am no longer ashamed. The pain is something different. It never goes away. I still long for family Fourth of July picnics with good food, laughter, and music; Thanksgiving dinners with the whole gang; and Christmas Eve at the house of the sister that I never had. I will always wish things had been different, but I take satisfaction in knowing that I've given it my all. Every day I try a little more.